THE ESSENTIAL NEW JERSEY DRIVER'S LICENCE HANDBOOK

Foreword

The Essential New Jersey driver's handbook is specifically written to ensure a remarkable success of all the driving test-takers by providing identical or the most closely related exam questions, followed by concise and quality lessons that aim to deliver a thorough understanding of the logic behind traffic signs, road marking and driving rules.

Our ultimate objective is to prepare you for the exam, making sure you do not experience any difficulty during the test. Be aware that these recommendations outline best practices for operating a car, but cannot cover every situation. You must rely on your judgement and adopt a safety-first mindset.

300 QUESTIONS AS SEEN ON TEST DAY

Each question is prepared carefully and in accordance with the exam pattern. These questions are closely related to the official examination questions. While the course includes the understanding of traffic rules and signs.

We write all of our questions using data directly from the most recent version of the Handbook.

We keep t___ ___ of ___ ___ ues and ___ ___, so ___ ___ f-date

C___ ___ ___ONS

High-quality and up-to-date lessons on traffic law, aiming at an easy understanding of the rules of the road and signals are available in this book. These lessons are made precise with the most advanced information and with regards to the most authentic sources.

EXPLAINED ANSWERS

Every question is provided with a detailed explanation of its right answer. This will enhance your knowledge and establish your mental basics. Knowing the information behind the answer would broaden your perception and intellect, helping you develop room for further yet easy apprehension.

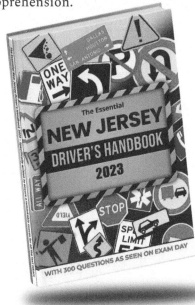

New Jersey Driver's License Handbook

ELS SERIES

ElS series identifies as an independent third party seller that aims to help test takers achieve their goals by providing **valuable lessons** that take inspiration from **The New Jersey Vehicle Code**, **Various official sources** and our **expertise.** Also, via **300 questions and answers** that are the most closest to the real exam questions.

We are by no means an **official source**, a **copy** or **our own version** of the **Official New Jersey Driver's Manual** nor **designed to replace it** in any shape or form.

ISBN: 9798840431214

CBMA31072205

THE ESSENTIAL NEW JERSEY DRIVER'S HANDBOOK

Contents   Page

THE ESSENTIAL NEW JERSEY DRIVER'S HANDBOOK

Contents   Page

The New Jersey Motor Vehicle commission (MVC) is in charge of developing driver competency in order to improve safety in the state of New Jersey. Along with this obligation, the MVC wishes to maintain all drivers' licenses valid for as long as it is safe for them to do so.

The MVC acknowledges that the freedom and mobility given by a driver's license is a vital aspect of most US residents quality of life. This is why an adequate testing system takes place to determine whether or not a person is capable of driving a specific type of vehicle. This multi-stage driver licensing process is known as the Graduated Driver License **GDL** Program. Giving the motorists a chance to gradually improve their driving skills and extend their practice driving time.

If you are a new resident and want to operate a motor vehicle in the state of New Jersey, you are required to purchase an examination permit within 60 days prior to becoming a permanent resident or when your out of state license expires whichever comes first.

In the state of New Jersey, there are 2 main types of Driving licenses. A commercial and non commercial DL. In the **non-commercial categories** there are different sub-types of licenses, each one of them qualifies candidates to drive a particular class of vehicles.

Basic Automobile License : Class D vehicles

By far the most crucial function of your driver's license is to inform law enforcement officials that you have received a driver's license in the state where you live and that you are legally permitted to drive a car.

The New Jersey driver's license as the picture shows is a white and maroon card made of plastic, that presents your name, photo and other identifying information. It has also an expiry date and needs to be renewed before it expires.

Class D License refers to a **basic non commercial license** and will allow you to drive a car, truck and a van. After meeting the eligibility requirements, which are being at least 18 years old and holding a probationary license for at least six months or hold a license from another state.

THE TESTING PROCESS

If you wish to get your driver's license in the state of New Jersey, you must follow the Motor Vehicle Commission MVC testing process, which consist of

1. **Provide the 6 points ID verification**

2. **Meeting the vision requirements**

3. **Passing the Knowledge test**

4. **Passing the Behind the wheel test**

6-Point ID Verification

Candidates need to provide documents that satisfy the 6 points ID verification. You can learn more about these documents via the MVC of New Jersey official website.

Vision Requirements

In order to get a drivers license in New Jersey candidates need to demonstrate the ability to meet the vision requirements when they apply for their first issued driver's license.

The vision test or screening test is given at the motor vehicle agencies offering driver testing services.

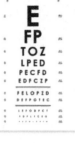

A representative will ask you to read lines of letters with both eyes open at first, then with each eye separately. Each phase of the exam will be guided by the employee.

For a non commercial license in this state, you need to have **20/50** vision acuity in one eye only with or without corrective lenses as the minimum vision required to be permitted the driving privilege with a minimum horizontal field of vision of 140°, your document will need to be signed by a licensed physician.

If you fail to pass this eye test you will be given a Vision Report (Form ST-14) found in all motor vehicle agencies. which must be completed by a licensed optometrist or ophthalmologist and submitted to the MVC.

This report will determine if you can be eligible to apply for a driver's license in the state of New Jersey and indicate if you need bioptic lenses for driving.

You may take the vision exam while wearing your glasses or contact lenses in case your driving license is currently limited for "**vision correction**."indicating that you need to wear your corrective lenses when behind the wheel.

Periodically, the MVC may require motorists to do a vision recheck for safety purposes.

Knowledge test

Passing the knowledge test is an important step in acquiring your driver's licence. This is a written examination that assesses your understanding of **Road signs** and **traffic laws and regulations** in the state of New Jersey.

You can schedule a **New Jersey's MVC Knowledge tests** via visiting the driver test centers, you must bring the 6 points document with you and purchase an examination permit. After that you can make an appointment for your knowledge test.

You can pass your knowledge test in some non English languages. Also, If the applicant cannot read in any language, he can ask for headphones to administer an oral test.

You can also use the service of a state approved interpreter . Nevertheless, you will be required to complete the test in an offered language first. If you fail to pass and feel you need an interpreter you can inform the MVC representative and clarify your situation.

The New Jersey's MVC knowledge test consists of

* **50 multiple-choice** questions

* you must have at least **40 correct answers** to pass.

The Exam Structure

The Road Signs Questions

This set of questions asses your understanding of the traffic signs. Candidates will be asked to indicate the meaning of certain road signs, signals and markers.

To add that the language of the road signs is English. Thus, you must show the ability to read and understand simple English such as used in highway traffic , road signs and directional signs.

The Rules of the Road Questions

This set of questions are about driver responsibility, knowledge of traffic laws and legislature in New Jersey such as the pointing system and the moving violations, and the best defensive driving decisions applicable to the type of license that you are applying for.

Road test

To demonstrate that you can safely operate a motor vehicle by adhering to the rules of the road, you will be evaluated on your driving skills in a road test administered by the MVC.

After passing the vision and knowledge test and you have practiced supervised driving for at least three to six months, in accordance to your age, you can then be eligible to pass your road test.

This test is available by appointments only. So that candidate can be served more efficiently. you can reserve an appointment by visiting any MVC Licensing Center or schedule it online via the NJ MVC official website.

Your vehicle condition can be a cause for disqualification, here are some of the most common causes of vehicle rejection by the MVC representative:

Missed seat belts, rear-view mirrors and/or driver doors who does not operate from the inside. broken or cracked window glass. Tinting on door windows. Poor brakes.

A Failed inspection of a vehicle, or driver not bringing inspection report issued by the inspection station to the road test area.

Fast engine idle or the vehicle dashboard displays a warning light indicating a problem.

Non functioning parking brake, brake lights, or signal lights and unsafe tires either damaged by a cut or badly worn.

Skills you must demonstrate during the driving test:

- **Parallel parking.** That is been said, Parking midway between 2 standards thus your vehicle is not more than 18 inches from the curb

- **Straight line backing/driving in reverse,** this involve Backing your vehicle for a distance of approximately 50 feet at a slow speed.

- **Stopping for signs and signals.**

- **Turn about.** Including narrow spaces using 3 point turns

- **Use of clutch,** if you have a manual car you must shift smoothly.

- **Passing and following other vehicles.**

- **Approaching intersections and corners.**

- **Yielding the right of way.**

  - **Maintaining good driving posture.(wearing the seatbelt)**

TRAFFIC SIGNAL RULES

Traffic at intersections may be controlled by utilizing *traffic signals* that employ green, yellow, and red lights. Whichever lane of traffic has **the right-of-way** is determined by the color of the light. A horizontal or a vertical traffic signal may be used.

 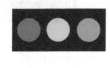

RED LIGHT

In the event of *solid red light,* drivers are required to come to a **full stop** (before the stop line or crosswalk). This rule applies at any intersection even where there is no crosswalk or stop line. To avoid accidents, drivers must wait for the green light before proceeding through the intersection.

Proceeding at a red light

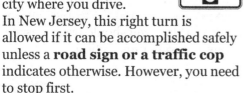

The first thing you need to know is if turning right at a red light is allowed in the city where you drive.

In New Jersey, this right turn is allowed if it can be accomplished safely unless a **road sign or a traffic cop** indicates otherwise. However, you need to stop first.

After stopping entirely, yield to other traffic and pedestrians on both your lane and the right lane crosswalk.

The only left turn authorized at a **red light** is into a one-way street from a one-way street unless a sign prohibits the turn. To make this turn, drivers must bring their vehicles to a full stop, and only then may they proceed.

FLASHING RED LIGHT

When facing a **flashing red light** put your vehicle to a complete stop, look for traffic from all sides of the intersection ahead, and if clear you can then proceed.

The easiest way to deal with flashing red lights is to treat them as stop signs, you should come to a full stop, check the intersection and yield right of way to others who got to the intersection before you and then proceed when the coast is clear.

GREEN ARROW WITH RED LIGHT

When confronted with a traffic signal that has both a green arrow and a red control light, drivers may pass through the intersection only in the direction indicated by the arrow without stopping.

YELLOW LIGHT

Yellow lights mean that you need to come to a full stop. Unless you are closer than one vehicle length to the intersection, than you are going to proceed through. do it defensively by covering the brakes, making sure you are scanning the intersection and that there aren't any road users. If you are farther back from the intersection than one vehicle length you need to come to a full stop.

FLASHING YELLOW LIGHT

flashing yellow light need to be treat it similarly to a yield sign. Continue cautiously after allowing pedestrians to cross and other vehicles to pass. You should slow down but not stop if there is no traffic on your way.

GREEN LIGHT

If the traffic control light is solid green, drivers may go through the intersection without stopping or slowing down if they drive within the speed limit, unless they must yield to **oncoming vehicles** when **turning left** or to **pedestrians in the crosswalk** when turning right or left.

When turning left, start off by getting into the leftmost of the lane to get ready to take the left-hand turn,

as you get closer to the intersection check that there is no oncoming traffic that you may obstruct and then also make sure that there are no pedestrians crossing or about to cross. While arriving at the intersection, check your rear-view mirror as well as your left side mirror and blind spots. You can then proceed to make the left turn in the correct manner.

FLASHING GREEN LIGHT

There is no need to stop when a flashing green traffic control signal is shown. Drivers may proceed and turn left or right without halting. Although the opposing traffic will face a red light, motorists must nonetheless yield to pedestrians or other vehicles that are legally at the junction.

GREEN ARROW WITH GREEN LIGHT

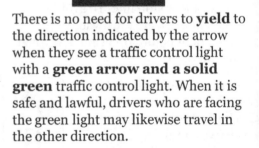

There is no need for drivers to **yield** to the direction indicated by the arrow when they see a traffic control light with a **green arrow and a solid green** traffic control light. When it is safe and lawful, drivers who are facing the green light may likewise travel in the other direction.

Remember: If you are approaching an intersection and the traffic lights are not working, you should treat is as a 4 way stop sign intersection.

There are some different types of yield signs that you may observe as per your state rules, some would even ask you to yield on solid green or yellow lights. Be cautious of those instructions.

PEDESTRIAN SIGNALS AND SIGNS

Pedestrian safety is a priority for the state of New Jersey. In order to anticipate the activities of others with whom you share the road, drivers must be familiar with pedestrian control signals. When it is safe to do so, pedestrians facing a traffic light with the word **"WALK"** or a similar symbol may cross the road. As long as the word or symbol appears, pedestrians may continue to cross and clear the intersection. **Countdown timers** may be seen on certain pedestrian signals to let pedestrians know how much time is left before the light changes.

If the text or symbol **"DON'T WALK"** appears on a traffic light, then a pedestrian must not cross the intersection.

 "WALK" is signalled by this pedestrian signal.

 "DON'T WALK" or **"WAIT"** signs for pedestrians

School zones or areas, playground zones or areas, school crossings, and pedestrian crossings all have yellow lights on a sign with a symbol to convey caution. It is mandatory for drivers to slow down to while the yellow lights are flashing and to yield or stop for pedestrians.

Pedestrian crossing signs with yellow lights.

Pedestrians must follow the regulations for the color of light they are facing at intersections with traffic control signals which lack pedestrian **WALK** and **DON'T WALK** signals.

• *Red light*; Do not cross the street at this time.

• *Yellow light*; Avoid entering the junction if you're already there.

• *Green light*; Proceed, Any designated or unmarked crosswalks may be used to cross the street.

Pedestrians should always look both ways before crossing the street.

Lane reversals send out a signal to other drivers.

These signals are used to regulate traffic flow in certain lanes. Reversible lanes, which alter traffic flow according to the time of day, are frequent users of this control. In one or more lanes, the signal(s) shift from a red X to a green arrow.

Solid red X:

Drivers must not enter or stay in a driving lane marked with a *solid red X.* An impending traffic signal is shown by this light. The green arrow indicates that the lane is safe to enter.

Downward pointing green arrow

Driving in the lane with the *downward-pointing green arrow* is authorized for drivers facing the arrow's direction.

ROAD SIGNS

Road signs all around the world come in various shapes and colors and memorizing the significance of each traffic sign can be challenging for some individuals.

However, studying them and understanding what each category is supposed to mean based on colors and shapes is a key point toward a quicker understanding of what you are being demanded to do for the optimal safety.

The traffic signs convey information to road users in 3 ways

1- the shape of the sign
2- the color of the sign
3- the symbols and/or writing on the sign

Color Coding

RED :
A Prohibition or a stop sign
The adoption of the red color on traffic signs is defined as a stop, a yield, or prohibition.

YELLOW :
Warning of a danger or a caution
Some signs are colored yellow, those should be perceived as a warning.

GREEN :
Announce traffic movement and directional instructions

The green signs are most recurrently presented on highways, freeways and mainly show travelers the directions, the exits, or the attractions.

ORANGE :
Temporary signs often alert travellers about construction and maintenance

The orange road signs refer to temporary conditions, these signs warn travelers of unusual situations like work zones ahead, detours, lane closures or traffic control people on the road. You should obey the instructions attentively as construction zones in most cases bring additional hazards.

WHITE :
Regulatory signs
The utilization of regulatory signs consists

of the implication or reinforcement of the laws regulating traffic. Regulations that apply at all times or within a predetermined window of time or place, either on streets or highways, or a general regulatory sign that governs public behaviour

BLACK :
Lane control signs
The lane control signs consist of managing the flow of traffic on certain lanes by permitting or prohibiting access to them.

The shapes of road signs:

Besides the colors, you can tell a lot about road signs by their shapes. They will give you your first piece of information. The shapes of a road signs that are the most commonly found are **triangles, diamond, rectangles and circles.**

1/ The actions inside the circle are permitted:

2/ The actions showed inside the circle are not Allowed

3/ These shapes often reveal that a school zone or a crosswalk ahead

4/ This Sign Show information or Instruction About Either Distance or Destination

5/ A Sign of a Regulatory Instruction Like speed limitation:

6/This sign reveal caution of hazard ahead on the road

7/ This Sign reveal places for fuel or Food, lodging or Assistance

8/ This Sign Inform You On a construction area or Temporary Work On the Road

9/ Reveals Lane control Ahead

REGULATORY SIGNS

The most prominent road signs are regulatory signs. The root word of regulatory is regulation. Regulation means law and if it's the law you must obey that sign.

Regulatory signs unlike the other classified road signs come in various shapes. However, the commonly used colors in this specific classification are red white and black.

Imperatively, drivers must have knowledge of these for the purposes of road tests to be successful either on the learner's or in on-road tests.

STOP SIGNS are eight-sided (octagonal shape) with a white border, and the word written on them is STOP. (Stop can be translated to Arrêt in French) and they stand for imperative stopping at the intersection where they are placed in.

YIELD SIGNS are three-sided (upside triangle) they have a wide red border and a white background. The yield sign indicates to the driver that they need to yield the right-of-way onto the road which they are entering or to any pedestrian and other traffic users

SPEED LIMITATIONS/ TRAFFIC MOVEMENT SIGNS are four-sided (rectangular shape) with a black border and white background. Mostly speed signs but can be about slow movement in the traffic. That is been said that drivers who drive slow should move over to the right lane so other drivers may pass for better traffic flow.

RAILWAY CROSSING SIGNS are shaped like an X with red borders and white background. Be cautious as you drive over a train track.

SCHOOL ZONE SIGNS are five-sided (pentagon in shape) Most of these signs are in neon green. These signs indicate that you are coming to a school zone, in New Jersey you need to drive with a speed limit of 25 MPH when you are in a school zone. Don't speed in a school zone! This infraction of the law can have major repercussions including an automatic fail on a road test.

PERMISSIVE SIGNS

These signs (a white square, a green circle) represent actions that are **permitted**.

Turn to the direction of the arrow only

Actions, objects and vehicles that are allowed on this lane

PROHIBITIVE SIGNS

These signs (a white square with a red circle along with a diagonal red bar) actions that are **prohibited**.

Taking the direction shown on these signs is not allowed

Other prohibitive signs

Pedestrians aren't allowed

Passing isn't allowed

Snow mobile aren't allowed

Bicycles arent allowed

Trucks aren't allowed

No dangerous goods are allowed

LANE USAGE SIGNS

LANE USAGE SIGNS are four-sided (rectangular shape) colored black and white, the arrows in them indicate which lane you are going to be in and which lane and what that lane is going to do whatever it's going left or right.

Usually, these lane marking signs are overhead of the lane and they are correlated with road markings .

Traffic direction lane

Proceed in direction of the arrow only:

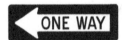 

Two way traffic

Divider ahead you need to keep right

Speed limit signs

The recommended maximum speed through the lane under normal conditions.

Reserved lanes

In some urban centers, to improve the safety and flow of designated vehicles, certain traffic lanes have been reserved for specific uses, indicated by traffic signs.

Double broken white lane lines and diamond symbols designate a with-flow reserved lane. If you are driving parallel to a diamond lane and need to turn right, you can enter the diamond lane but you must turn right at the next intersection. If you are turning right onto a street with a diamond lane in the curb lane, you must turn into that lane, then signal, check and change lane lanes out of the Diamond lane into the adjacent lane as soon as it is safe to do so.

Always be watchful and respect the rights of the cyclists using the diamond lanes.

high occupancy vehicle lanes or HOV lanes, usually located on the inside left lane are dedicated to car poolers with a minimum of 2 people per vehicle during peak travel hours to reduce traffic congestion, during the remaining hours, the HOV lane will function as any other lane does on the freeway. The HOV lane is delineated with distinct and unique pavement markings. Permanent signage will be used to explain HOV lane usage.

The least occupancy state revolves around 2 to 3 occupants. According to certain laws, vehicles consisting of motorbikes, emergency vehicles, charter buses or law enforcement cars may be exempted.

HOV Lanes Usage: By law, a driver is allowed to use the HOV lane only in case there are a minimum of two people in the vehicles as listed below:

Cars, lightweight trucks, or vans, such as commercial trucks.

The below-listed vehicles have no restrictions on the HOV lanes:

Mass transit including **Buses, taxis or limousines** that are licensed. all emergency vehicles, motorbikes, certain plug in hybrid, alternative fuel are exempted from the HOV restrictions.

CONSTRUCTION SIGNS

The **construction zone** signs are orange with a black stroke and the symbols or writings on them are black. Most of the time rectangular or diamond in shape. Therefore a construction sign warns you of **hazards** and **obstructions** on the roadway and often these are temporary conditions.

In construction sites, signs work in concert with many other apparatus to warn you and guide you safely through the construction zone: Pylons, flaggers, signs and sometimes pilot vehicles will all direct you out of the constructions zone. So be aware of all those apparatus to get you safely and avoid the hazards and obstructions that present themselves as temporary conditions.

Pylons on construction zones are orange and black striped, you can see in construction areas most of the time diggers that are a characteristic of construction zones.

Construction zones also can be surrounded by fences, which creates a distinct physical barrier between traffic and construction zones. Below are some of the warning road signs related to road construction:

SCHOOL ZONE & AREAS

The first school sign gives you an advanced notice that there is a school in and around the area and if there are children present on the roadway. You need to slow down, reduce your speed, do not pass or attempt to pass vehicles travelling in the same direction and use extra caution.

In New Jersey, the speed in school zone areas is set at **25 MPH** unless a road sign says otherwise. Moreover, school times are generally between 8 am and 5 pm during school days. Note that this information may vary in some areas or towns.

You may also find signs that alert you of school zone crossings with road markings that accompany this sign. You have to completely stop and let pedestrians cross regardless of how many lanes of traffic, in this province as well as in some other jurisdictions.

RAILWAY CROSSING SIGNS

One of the reasons why railway crossing is an important compound of driving knowledge is the danger that trains evolve as they can't keep a steady schedule. You need to know also that trains have always the right-of-way. And that at night the risk of an incident multiplies as drivers don't have a clear vision so drive with extra caution in those areas .

ADVANCED WARNING SIGNS

Many railway crossings have warning signs that warn you beforehand that there is going to be a railway crossing, there might be road markings. All railway crossings that intersect with roadway have advanced traffic control signs, signals or even flashing lights and gates .

TRAFFIC REGULATION SIGNS

The second most common signs are the cautionary or advisory signs they are usually four-sided (diamond shape, rectangular shape). They have a yellow background and the symbols and writings on them are black.

Hazard marker object will warn you of hazards and obstructions on the roadway and on which side to pass or whether you can pass on either the right or left.

Turn or curve ahead

Sharp turn Right

Sharp turn Left

Curves right

Road curves right

Road turns Left/right

Winding road

Changing road conditions

Hill   **Bumps**

   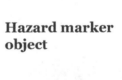

Pavement ends   **Slippery when wet**

Rumble strips **Falling rocks**

Hazard marker object

Left   Right

Chevron sign indicates a sharp bend in the road

Narrow roadways ahead

Road narrows both sides

Narrow passage

Left lane narrows to right

Right lane narrows to left

Left lane ends

Right lane ends

Divided highway begins   **Divided highway ends**

SPEED LIMITATION

The recommended maximum speed through the curve under normal conditions

Crossing ahead

Animal crossing

Pedestrian crossing

Bicycle crossing **Railway crossing**

Intersection ahead

Hidden road left

Hidden road right

Y intersection

T intersection

Merging traffic

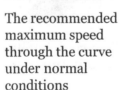

Roundabout

There is nothing to worry about in case you were asked to pull over and received a traffic ticket in the state of New Jersey. Even though it is not very easy to get a moving violation, there are certain ways through which you can clear the traffic ticket process smoothly and promptly as well as keep your driving record clean.

In case you are pulled over due to a speeding ticket or any other traffic violation, there are certain things that you should expect to take place. First, an officer will ask you to show him your driving license, registration, as well as your proof of insurance. All of these items are considered to be ticket-able offenses, therefore it is vital to carry these documents with you whenever you are in your vehicle.

If you have any further questions or need any clarification you can ask the officer respectfully to explain the process furthermore for you.

When the officer gives you a ticket to sign and you do not agree with his decision, do not extend the contact by arguing with him. Instead you can seek to contest the decision in court via the established legal channels. You can also ask to speak to an officer's supervisor if you believe that the officer acted inappropriately.

Signing a traffic ticket **doesn't mean** an **admission of guilt. Nevertheless,** convictions are added to your driving record.
If you refuse to sign a traffic ticker, this may lead to your arrest.

New Jersey's Point system

A lot of people think that they have a right to drive. While driving is actually a privilege in most states including New Jersey. This why a point system can affect your driving privilege.

Demerit points are added to your driving record upon convictions of certain moving violations.

A conviction of the following offences will lead to adding **2 points** to your driving record:

- Not yielding the right of way to a pedestrian
- Failing to obey a traffic signal
- Proceeding through a stop or yield sign
- Driving in the wrong way on a one-way street
- Slow driving and causing traffic block
- Exceeding the speed limit from 1 to 14 mph
- Failing to stop for a traffic stoplight
- Moving violation

The following offences carry three points or more

- Prohibited U-turns: 3 points
- Passing in a no passing zone: 4 points
- Disobeying right or left turn: 3 points
- Reckless driving: 5 points
- Speeding over 15 to 29 mph: 4 points
- Speeding over 30 mph: 5 points
- Attempting or passing a stopped school bus: 5 points
- An accident resulting in personal injury: 8 points

According to the New Jersey MVC, Up to 3 points will be automatically deducted from your driving record every year if the driver goes without any violation/suspension. However, your driving record will never be reduced below zero.
To add, Under New Jersey state law, your driving privileges will be suspended if you have **12 or more points** on your record.

LAWS GOVERNING NEW JERSEY DRIVING PRIVILEGE

Type of offenses

infraction: This is what covers the entire fundamental New Jersey traffic violations. From running a red light to speeding, all types of traffic violations.

Misdemeanor: This is considered a very serious driving offense. These may include over speeding, driving under the influence of alcohol or drugs, driving without having any license or with a revoked license, etc.

Driving with a suspended license

Driving with a suspended license or registration will lead to the following :

• **For a 1st conviction,** you will be Fined $500 and a maximum of 6 months additional suspension of your license or registration.

• **For a 2nd conviction:** you will be fined $750, up to 5 days of jail and 6 months additional suspension of your license or registration n.

• **For a 3rd Conviction** you will face a fine of $1,000, a ten days in jail and up to 6 months additional suspension of your license or registration.

Irresponsible driving

Committing an offense of irresponsible driving that can endangers an individual or a property will lead to the payment of a minimum fine of $50 or even more than $150 for a 1stconviction. For a second conviction you will be fined $100-$250.And not less than $200 or more than $500 for a 3rd subsequent conviction.

Hit-and-run

A hit-and-run conviction causing bodily injury or death will lead to a fine of between $2,500-$5,000 and or up to 6 months of jail.

65 mph zone offences and failing to comply

You will get a double fined if you over speed (exceeding with 10 mph) above the posted speed limit or other moving violations in a 65 mph speed area. Some offenses include racing on a public highway, refusal to comply with an officer's request, failure to obey traffic signs or signals, failure to comply with rules for passing another vehicle, failure to obey road markings, failure to observe distance between vehicles, and careless driving

Important legislature of the new jersey driving privilege

• If you want to operate a motor vehicle in the State of New Jersey you need to carry a valid driver license or permit, a proof of insurance and vehicle registration cards.

• if you want to Change your address , you are required to report this to the MVC within 1 week after moving.

• If you legally change your name you need to report the change to the MVC within 2 weeks.

• Moving to the state of New Jersey with a valid out of state license require you to apply for a NJ license within 60 days for a non commercial license and 30 days for a commercial driver license or before the current license expires. whichever is sooner. A driver with a non expired license from another country is allowed to drive with it for up to a 1 year in New Jersey.

• Any four point offenses and accumulating four points in one year

LAW ENFORCEMENT STOP

A Law enforcement stop occurs when a police officer suspect a **traffic violation** or a **criminal violation**. During this process make sure that the police officer acknowledges that you have noticed him and switch on your right-turn signal and when it is safe to do so, come to a full stop. Even if you're in the carpool/HOV lane, go entirely to the right shoulder.

1. Turn off your engine, stop talking on the phone or maybe turn off the radio and lower your window so the officer can communicate with you.
2. Unless the police tell you otherwise, stay in your vehicle. If the officer ask you to exit the vehicle, keep your hand visible and stand in the direction where the officer ask you to do.
3. After you've been pulled over and the police have made contact with you, roll down your windows.
4. Before the police make contact with you, make sure your hands and the hands of all passengers are visible. This might be on your wheel, dashboard, and let the officers know if you have any weapon.

NEW JERSEY'S SPEED LAWS

Most people think it is fine to drive with the flow of traffic. However this is not true, the flow of traffic is never a standard of the lawful speed in every circumstances. In fact, there a 4 major speed laws, that you need to obey as a driver:

The basic speed law

The **basic speed law** is the most common of all and states that you should not exceed a safe speed on a roadway based on weather and road conditions, that is been said, that driving within the speed limit can be too fast in the presence of those conditions.

Statutory speed law

The statutory or prima facie speed law mandates a statutory speed limit in areas where speed signs may not be posted, nevertheless they should be known and followed by default. In the state of New Jersey the statutory speed laws are as follow :

- **25 MPH (miles per hour)** while driving in school zones, business and residential areas.
- **35 MPH (miles per hour)** while driving on suburban business and residential areas.
- **50 MPH (miles per hour)** on non posted rural roadways.
- **55 MPH (miles per hour)** while driving on certain state highways and interstates as posted.
- **65 MPH (miles per hour)** while driving in certain interstate highways as posted.

The maximum speed law

The maximum speed law basically means you are not allowed to exceed the speed limit posted in a road sign.

New Jersey's slow driving law

In order to not impede or interrupt the normal flow of traffic, drivers are not allowed to drive at such slow speed in the state of New Jersey. Minimum speed limit signs can be found in some highways, in case you can't drive with the minimum required speed you need to take an alternate route.

In two or more ways roads where traffic is moving the same direction, slower vehicles need to use the right hand lane. That is been said, you are not allowed to drive too slowly in the passing lane (most left lane).

Driving under the influence of alcohol or any drug that can impair your driving ability is often referred to as DUI and is illegal in the state of New Jersey. As it can lead to serious repercussions, such as death. Technically, any blood alcohol concentration level **(BAC) above 0.08%** is considered an illegal BAC, thus prohibit you from operating a motor vehicle.

In the state of New Jersey, you need to be at least 21 years old to purchase, possess or consume alcohol. Under age motorists found with a BAC of .01% or higher while driving a motor vehicle will lead to severe consequences.

Implied consent

Driving in the state of New Jersey mean automatically that the state have your full consent to test your blood breath or urine in case a law enforcement officer suspects that you are driving under the influence on New Jersey roadways.

If a driver refuses to take a breath test, the law enforcement officers are allowed to detain and brought the driver to a hospital, where the hospital staff can draw blood. he is also a subject to a fine of $1,000 per year for three years.

A conviction of refusing a breath test can lead to the loss of the driving privilege, in accordance to the number of past offenses.

Also, refusals in connection with a first offense will result in the same outcome until an ignition interlock device has been installed on the driver's vehicle.

Consequences of DUI

Convictions of a DUI offense will lead to mandatory penalties, for a 1st conviction of DUI With a BAC of 0.08% or more but less than 0.10% , you will get a fine of $250-$400, 12h to 48h in Intoxicated Driver Resource Center with paying a fee, up to a one month of imprisonment, $1,000 annual surcharge for three years and other penalties.

For a 1st conviction of driving with a BAC of over than 0.1 % you will be subject to a fine of a minimum of $300 up to $500 in fines, 12h to 48h in Intoxicated Driver Resource Center with paying a fee, up to a one month of imprisonment, $1,000 annual surcharge for three years and other penalties.

For a 1st conviction of driving with a BAC of over than 0.10 % while being under 21 years old you will be subject to 30- to 90-day suspension of driving privilege, 15 to 30 days community service and participation in an Intoxicated Driver Resource Center or alcohol education program

Ignition interlock device

Under the New Jersey state intoxicated driving statute, A convicted driver of a DUI is required to install an ignition interlock device in whichever vehicle he operates the most (owns, leases, or principally operates) during and after the entire period for which their driving privilege is suspended.

This device will be attached to the vehicle with a built-in breathalyzer in order to prevent the engine from starting if the driver's blood alcohol concentration is over the 0.05% allowed.

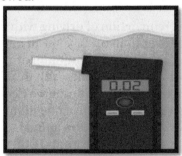

1st DUI conviction with less than 0.15 percent BAC will lead to the Installation of ignition interlock device for 3 months to 1 year from the date of driving privilege restoration.

1st DUI conviction with a 0.15% BAC or higher/ Refusing a

Breath Test conviction will lead to Installing an ignition interlock device in your vehicle

A. During the suspension period .
B. For 9 to 15 months starting from the date of driving privilege restoration.

2nd or Subsequent DUI conviction/ 2nd Refuse to submit to a breathing test will lead to The installation of an ignition interlock device on your vehicle

A. During the suspension period
B. For 2 to 4 years starting from your driving privilege restoration date.

Conviction of a DUI while you are driving a minor :

Conviction of a driving under the influence offense while having a minor who is under 18 years old, as a passenger mean that you are guilty of a disorderly person's offense.

This will lead to a driving privilege suspension for a maximum of 6 months and performing community services for up to 5 days.

Intoxicated Driver Resource Center

New Jersey legislature requires that any driver charged with a DUI need to be detained at an IDRC. The IDRC will evaluate offenders and determine the appropriate treatment. Those deemed in need of treatment will be referred to a provider for a treatment program.

The state of New Jersey has a compulsory financial responsibility law requiring all vehicles registered in the state of New Jersey to have an insurance coverage. The purpose of this law is to ensure that you can be financially responsible for any collision in which you are involved regardless of fault and to remove irresponsible drivers from the road.

As a licensed driver, you must keep this evidence of insurance in your car, truck, motorbike, or other vehicles at all times. In fact, if you cannot show proof of insurance during a law enforcement stop or in a collision situation, officers have the right to take your vehicle away, and you license may get suspended by the MVC.

If you allow another person to drive a vehicle that you own, you must still proof financial responsibility required by law. The most common method is maintaining liability insurance with an insurance company.

Liability insurance coverage

The basic New Jersey auto-insurance policy is **liability insurance.** This coverage pays for damages when accidentally injuring someone or damaging another vehicle or property in an auto accident.

Keep in mind that this part of the policy only pays for the other person's injuries and damages to their vehicle and not your own.

New Jersey's minimum liability insurance requirements are as follows:

1. $15,000 per person for injury or death
2. $30,000 per accident for all injuries
3. $5,000 for property damage
4. $15,000 per person for personal injury protection

The best amount of coverage will depend on you and your budget. most insurance companies also provide a card or other documents other than the policy itself that you can use as a evidence of financial responsibility.

There are minimal standards for the quantity of insurance you have on the vehicle and yourself as the driver if you wish to get the liability insurance.

A comparative fault law

New Jersey is a comparative fault state. Which means that faults are assigned proportionately in accordance to the percentage of fault that has been assigned.

This indicates that different drivers may share fault and receive awards based on the amount of fault that they are given.

Drivers who are found at least 50% at-fault for a collision in this state will not recover any damage nor compensation.

Reportable traffic collisions

A reportable traffic accident is any type of a collision where the damage is $500 or more, or if a person involved get any level of injury or dies from the collision. You must report the accident to the local police department if it occurred in town, in case its outside of the town report it to the state patrol.

It is the Department of Public Safety's policy that a law enforcement officer will immediately respond to the scene when he is notified of a crash.

In case it is a personal accident you are encouraged to call 911 after the crash has occurred, and you can fill out the Personal Report of Accident form later. That is been said, there are no reporting requirements.

Fraudulent actions to avoid

Lying on purpose in your insurance application.

The claim of previous damages with the damages of a new accident.

The submission of health care claims after a person injured in an accident has recovered.

The claim of a non-existent injury and the claim of an accident that did or didn't happen.

If a driver is convicted of fraudulent action such ad lying on insurance applications and claims forms can be penalized by a fine of up to $5,000, or imprisonment for up to 3 years, or even both.

Conviction of an automobile insurance crime is subject to losing your driving privilege for one year according to new jersey state laws.

THE RIGHT-OF-WAY RULE

There is no denying, the fact that there are high chances of a collision occurring at intersections. As we don't know who must move and who needs to yield. The **Right-Of-Way** is a crucial rule that defines when and who should proceed first in such situations.

Rules of the road are generally determined via the signs, signals and mostly with **the location of your vehicle** with reference to other vehicles. Thus, the **Right-of-way** rule requires one person to yield and allow the other to proceed in accordance with his position on the road and the signs that must be followed. However, in the absence of traffic control signals, signs or traffic cops, it can be presumed by the following hierarchy:

1/ Pedestrians first
2/ First vehicle to arrive
3/ Vehicles on the right
4/ Straight through traffic over turning vehicles
5/ Right turning traffic over left-turning

Despite having the complete edge of the situation, you are still expected to demonstrate a responsible attitude by doing whatever it takes to avoid accidents. **A golden rule** is that the right-of-way is never taken it is always given.

Note that directions and instructions given by a police officer in an intersection or in general must be followed over traffic signs or signals.

INTERSECTIONS

Driving at intersections is a very important component of the rules of the road lessons, this is because more than 40% of crashes happen at intersections, and it's the one place that you're most likely to encounter and cross paths with vulnerable road users (pedestrians, cyclists, motorcycle riders, scooters and skaters).

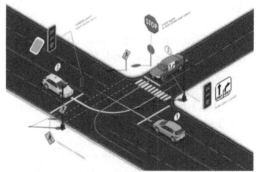

An intersection could be defined as a junction or a stretch of the roadway in which 2 or more roads converge, diverge meet or cross paths. An intersection can be a crossroad also known as a four-way intersection or three-way intersection and can be a T-junction or a Y-junction in appearance as well.

When you come up to an intersection, it is imperative to **scan** not only forward through the intersection but also have to scan the cross traffic and look for pedestrians at the cross traffic, because if you misjudge the pedestrians they could hold you up in the intersection and you can consequently block it. Thus you need to drive slowly and you need to be calm and relaxed, that way you can interpret traffic patterns and predict the individual actions of other road users.

Vehicle signals, slowing down and hesitation are the common signs of a turning vehicle on the roadway. Pedestrians on the edge of the road communicate to drivers that they are preparing to cross the street. Driving at the intersections involves shoulder checks as well. to check for the vehicles coming from behind and to check out blind spots.

One of the most important rules of driving is to never change lanes in an intersection. Because you are being unpredictable when you are making sudden turns through the intersection or the roundabout (which is also considered an intersection), you are not exercising the skills and techniques of the safest driving practices. So even if there is no legislation presented for that, make sure to never change lanes in the intersection as it significantly increases the chance of being involved in a risk.

The challenge for brand new drivers is differentiating between controlled and uncontrolled intersections, because these two types of intersection have different right-of-way rules, and for new drivers it poses a challenge .

CONTROLLED INTERSECTIONS

Controlled intersections rely on stop signs, yield signs, and traffic lights for traffic management.

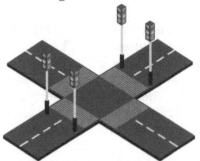

Carefully drive through the intersection at a normal speed and obey all the instructions.

Controlled by a stoplight

In case the light is green for a certain period of time, you need to prepare yourself to stop if it switches to yellow.

With that being said, if you are not able to stop safely due to the reason that you are already very close, in that scenario, you need to drive through the intersection with extreme care. When the stoplight is red, you should bring your vehicle to a complete halt. You need to wait until the red light turns green before proceeding.

In case you want to turn left in a controlled intersection via stoplights where you've got along line of cars coming at you. When the light is green (eventually it will be on both directions) you need to put your front steer tires on the front crosswalk line, that's where you need to wait. And **anticipate the**

gap, so when the opposite direction traffic is cleared meet the gap, shoulder check and then left turn.

Controlled by a sign

Stop Sign: At stop signed intersections, you need to bring the vehicle stop at the correct stopping, and if you can't see the cross-traffic or you can't see the intersection, then you need to creep forward and eventually treat it as a yield, therefore, give the right-of-way to other road users.

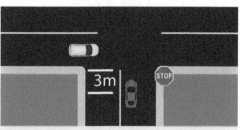

Note that there should be enough room (3 meters) for the pedestrians to walk by easily.

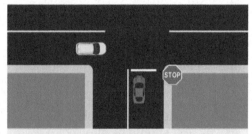

When the stop line is indicated, stop your vehicle completely. You are good to go when given enough room for the pedestrians to walk by safely and the way is clear

Do not cross a marked crosswalk when coming to a stop.

In case there is no crosswalk or a stop line near the intersection, you should stop before the intersecting roads at a distance of at least three meters or ten feet.

Two-way Stops intersection

You will most likely find a two-way stop intersection in the residential areas. There is going to be a major thoroughfare through those areas and all the minor roads must have stop signs.

Two-way intersections are different than three-way intersections or all-way intersections. While arriving position your vehicle to the right and yield to vehicles coming.

You should know that pedestrians have the right of way first, after **that major roads have the right of way over minor roads**, and then the other rules apply straight through traffic over turning traffic, right-turning over left-turning.

However, a lot of people are confused and think that the left-turning traffic is going to go first if they arrive first at two-way stop sign intersections. Which is not true for this specific situation.

Three and Four-Way Stops:

A 3-way stop simply means a T-intersection, and every point of entry to the intersection at the T has to come to a stop before proceeding through the intersection. the same rules apply for 4-way intersections and anything above a 2-way intersection.

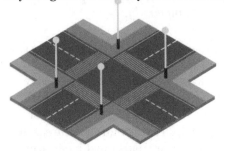

The **right-of-way rule** for this type of intersection is different from the 2-way stop intersection:

Pedestrians first
The first vehicle to arrive
Vehicles on the right
Straight through traffic over turning vehicles
Right turning traffic over left-turning

There is a couple of information that you need to know particularly when 4-way intersections are busy.

Most 4-ways stops are going to have stop lines, so it's not going to be confusing about where you stop. Because these intersections tend to be busy they have crosswalks for pedestrians and you are asked to give them the right-of-way first and do not crowd pedestrians for the purpose of a road test or driving in general.

that is been said, You need to hold the brake until you come to a complete stop behind the stop line and before the crosswalk. After that wait until there is one lane of traffic between you and pedestrians.

After that wait until there is one lane of traffic between you and pedestrians. As well as when they are busy they take turns, it's almost as if your lane of traffic goes and then the cross-traffic goes.

The term "courtesy corners" is used for such an intersection where traffic signs are located at all corners. All vehicles that approach the intersection should stop and establish a sense of courtesy following caution.

This means that the vehicle which arrives first should be allowed to proceed faster as well. Similarly, in case both vehicles reach the intersection at an equal time, courtesy demands the vehicles on the right to proceed first. But, if the other can proceed safely first, then there is no objection to doing so.

If two vehicles are proceeding straight, the two vehicles can proceed at the same time. And two left-turning vehicles across from one another can proceed at the same time.

As well as straight-through vehicles have the right of way over turning vehicles. nevertheless, proceed with caution because you may not know whether that other vehicle is going to proceed through the intersection.

Yield Sign: Yield signs at intersections are not a common thing in residential areas. However, you can encounter some of them, especially in T-intersections.

But most of the time you are going to find yield signs at slip lanes or roundabouts. That's where this sign is the most prolific.

If you approach an intersection with a yield sign you have to give the right of way to other road users in the intersection if they are present. That means if there are other vehicles or road users at the intersection, you have to stop and wait for them to clear the intersection.

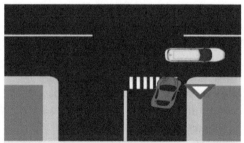

The right defensive position is to creep to the intersection in order to have a clear vision and to drive at a speed that permits you to stop with ease to prevent collisions.

UNCONTROLLED INTERSECTIONS

You will find uncontrolled intersections usually in the quieter residential areas where there is not a lot of traffic. they can also be found in some industrial areas and some rural areas as well. due to their unique situation, uncontrolled intersections have no traffic control signals or signs.

Yielding the right-of-way in an uncontrolled intersection

You should as well scan the intersection very concisely to see if the other paths don't have any signs or lights. In case you have reached an uncontrolled intersection at close to the same time, the vehicle who actually reached the intersection last is the driver who must yield the right of way.

This is critical if you fail to slow down eventually be ready to stop at any moment and check for traffic in both directions at an uncontrolled intersection you can fail your road test.

If you arrive at the same time, the vehicles on the left must always yield the right of way to the vehicles on the right. The driver on the right must still pay attention to avoid collisions.

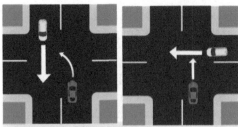

The blue car needs to yield to the **white car** in this case

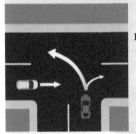

The white car needs to yield to the **Blue car** in case of both paths in this T shaped intersection

Be extremely cautious in this situation as the drivers that are going straight through (white) make the assumption that they do have the right of way incorrectly.

The Intersections Must be Kept Cleared

You should not attempt to proceed in an intersection unless you can fully clear it. In a situation when traffic is backed up at an intersection, avoid a traffic jam or any accident until the intersection and crosswalk is clear.

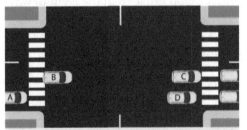

In this case, **A** is in the correct position. **B** has blocked the crosswalk. However, the **C & D** vehicles have used poor judgement

Pedestrian crossing in controlled and uncontrolled intersections

In general, pedestrians have the right-of-way to cross regardless of the type of intersection, crosswalks or direction.

At pedestrian crossings and school crossings with a crosswalk, cede the right-of-way and wait for pedestrians to cross the road.

Keep in mind that signalling does not provide you with the right of way to ensure that the path is clear.

Do not blindly follow traffic at intersections

If your view is obstructed by a large vehicle, logging truck or a commercial vehicle you need to be cautious and not follow the movement of the traffic flow, mainly because you wont be able to see around and forward, particularly when there is no enough space as you get closer.

you may find that when you proceed you cannot see the traffic light and you may enter a red light which is an automatic fail during your driving test. Thus you need to let a large.

Hence you need to let a safe distance between you and the large vehicle that gives you a proper view.

CHANGING AND MERGING LANES

Merging and changing lanes can sometimes be a stressful task for some road users. Whenever you change lanes from one marked lane to another you must give the right of way to vehicles already in that lane or line of traffic. This includes merging into freeway traffic , you need to indicate that you are switching lanes via your vehicles signals in order to change lanes when there is a safe gap in traffic .

When the lane in front of you is blocked, you must indicate and give the right of way.

Zip merging is when two lanes of traffic merge into one, on a road where there are no road marking , you must give the right of way to any vehicle which has any part of its vehicle ahead of yours.

As you are proceeding on onto a roadway, you may see a merging lane sign, so you need to shoulder-check to make sure nobody is trying to sneak past you, you need also to signal and stay to the top side of the curve.

To access a highway or freeway, check the cross traffic and turn onto the acceleration lane. you are not onto the acceleration lane until you pass **the continuity lines.**

ROUNDABOUTS AND TRAFFIC CIRCLES

Roundabouts are circular forms of intersections that are specifically designed to enhance the safety and flow of traffic. there are in fact several benefits to them:

First and foremost, there are fewer points of conflict for turning traffic in roundabouts, thus fewer collisions. And the next thing is that they facilitate a higher level of traffic flow through the intersection and finally the other benefit is that there is less noise because there are fewer cars that are actually coming to a full stop and accelerating away from the intersection.

In North America traffic in roundabouts travel in a counterclockwise direction. vehicles that enter the intersection should yield to the traffic present in the roundabout. In other words, the vehicle on the right must yield to the car on the left when in the circle. . To add that in some intersections, there are arrows to indicate in which direction the roundabout is flowing. And the recommended speed at the roundabout is 20 MPH.

Nevertheless in countries like the UK and Australia where they drive on the left side of the road traffic will flow in a clockwise direction, so be aware of that.

Single-lane roundabout

When you are coming up to the roundabout, you have to be prepared to stop and go at the same time. in other words, you have to scan well ahead at the roundabout and determine if there is traffic in there that you need to yield to, or traffic that's about to move into the roundabout that is going to impede your movement through the roundabout. Also, it is important to put your signals to indicate which direction of the road are you taking, in case you are going straight forward you are not asked to do so.

Exiting a single lane roundabout :

However when you are exiting put your signal in advance to alert the following traffic. For example, if you are exiting from a left route or making a U-turn make a left signal. Since the other drivers would understand that you need to leave the circle, the chances of an accident should be minimal. Leave the signal on until you successfully and safely leave the circle.

Multi-lane roundabouts

If you have a multi-lane roundabout you need to think of it as a conventional intersection. If you are going to make a left-hand turn you want to be in the left-hand lane and vice versa, if you want to make a right-hand turn you need to be in the right-hand lane as you are approaching the roundabout.

Exiting the Multi-lane roundabout:

In case you are travelling in the right-hand lane, your intention must be to make a right turn or to proceed through the roundabout. On the other hand, if you are willing to make a U-turn or exit on the left you must be in the left-hand lane. Remember that same as the conventional intersections ,do not change lanes on the roundabout because it will obstruct and slow the traffic flow and you are being unpredictable, therefore, the risk of collision increases.

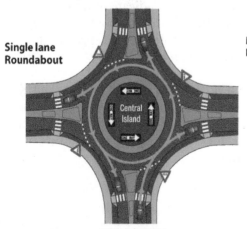

Single lane
Roundabout

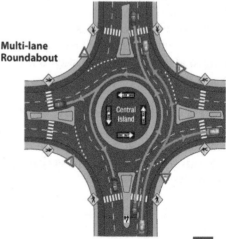

Multi-lane
Roundabout

Pavement markings work in tandem with traffic signs and stoplight signals to provide crucial details regarding the traffic flow and where you may and may not go to ensure everyone's safety.

Concrete patterns (straight or broken line) Different colors and numbers (white or yellow) (single or double) play a major role in separating lanes of traffic, displaying the change in roadways, identifying pedestrian movement, highlighting obstructions, and warning when it is unsafe to overtake, change lanes or make a U-turn.

Yellow line markings separate traffic moving in the opposite direction, mark the center of a roadway and on divided highways they mark the left edge. On the other hand, **White lane markings** separate traffic moving in the same direction and mark the edge of a roadway.

A Solid line marking indicates restricted movement, which means that crossing the solid line to pass or change is prohibited.

Broken line marking means that crossing the broken line to pass or change lanes is permitted.

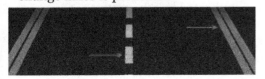

Yellow Lane markings

A **broken yellow line** mark a passing zone, you may drive on the left lane to pass other vehicles, only when it is safe to do so.

Solid yellow lines, single or double to the left of your lane indicate that passing is risky and therefore **not allowed**.

A solid yellow line and a broken yellow line together mean that passing is allowed for drivers who have the broken line on their side of the road. However, passing is not allowed for the driver with the solid yellow line on their side of the road.

White Lane markings

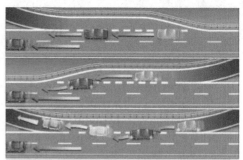

When you notice continuity lines on your left side, it usually implies that the lane you're in is coming to **an end or departing**, and you'll need to change lanes to continue in your present path. Continuity lines on your right indicate that your lane will remain untouched.

Solid white line means that you can't cross the line, expect to avoid an accident. If it's a double solid white line you can't cross the line under no circumstances.

Note that a **normal** single solid white line indicate that crossing the line is discouraged and not prohibited.

A stop line is a single white line painted across the road. It indicates that you need to stop just a bit before the line. If there is no stop line. You should **stop**, whether it is marked or not.

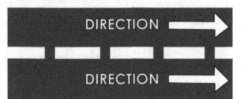

Broken or dashed white lines mean that you can cross the lines when it is safe to do so, and that the traffic is going in the same direction.

From solid to dashed means that when you get to this point you can change lanes.

You may only go in the direction indicated by the arrow.

Left turning center lanes

Solid and broken yellow lines are also used for **center left turning lanes**, these are often on main thoroughfare in the center of the road that let you turn from a major road on to a minor road. remember that the center lane is for left turns only, it is not a passing lane and make sure to position your vehicle well on that lane so you wont block traffic.

There can is also two-way left turn center lane, which means traffic from both directions can use that lane for left turns, and you don't need to worry about collisions because if there is a left turning vehicle coming from the opposite direction they are going to be back a fair distance.

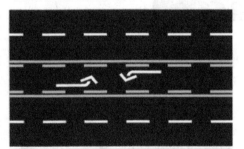

Two-way left turning center lane

Symbols

These symbols are utilized on the pavement to aid road users. These can also be used by themselves for the purpose of alerting the driver to guide or regulate the traffic. These markings may involve:

Arrows: The movements of vehicles that are permitted in a particular lane is indicated by the arrows.

Diamond markings

Diamonds lanes are a restricted **lanes**, that's been said, only certain vehicles meeting the posted criteria on the sign are allowed to travel on those specific **lanes**. These criteria can be either related to the type of vehicle or certain times and dates in which they can use the lane in question usually in the rush hours.

Shared used lanes or **Sharrows** are used to alert motorists that bicyclists may occupy the travel lane. They can also help bicyclists maintain a safe lane position. cyclists should ride **one metre** from the curb to avoid debris and sewer grates. While you should leave at least **one meter** between your vehicle and cyclists.

Diamond A lane reserved for bicycles

Sharrows This symbol marks a lane shared by motorists and bicyclists.

41

Pavement marking in railway crossing

Trains always have the right-of-way. This is not only because a very long distance is required by the trains to come to a stop. But also, trains don't have a clear schedule and are not as maneuverable as normal vehicles.

Railway crossings in most cases are marked with the X symbol. They may also carry electrical as well as mechanical warning devices such as flashy lights.

X markings

X markings indicate that you are coming to railway crossing, in case you may need to stop and give the right-of-way to a train, make sure to stop before the X marking.

Painted island

Yellow lines on the painted island indicate that they separate opposing lanes of traffic thus it is prohibited to drive on the painted island. In fact you should consider it as a solid yellow lines. So stay on the right and do not drive on it.

The purpose of these painted islands is to create a buffer of space between two opposing lanes of traffic as there is a transition that is often two lanes traveling in one direction which goes to third lane that becomes a left hand turning lane.

Accessible parking via permit

If you are an accessible parking permit holder, you must always display your current permit on the dashboard or sun visor of the vehicle you are travelling in, so the permit number and expiry date is clearly visible.

The only person that is allowed to use the permit for parking is the person who's name is on the permit. If another person did so he may face a penalty of up to $5,000 and his permit can be seized.

Numerous roadway users utilize New Jersey roadways, including pedestrians, motorcyclists, cyclists, large trucks, buses, and agricultural equipment. Be mindful of other drivers on the road, their speeds, and the amount of space they require.

Whenever you follow another vehicle, you need to allow enough space to stop safely in case the vehicle you are following brakes suddenly.

A safe following distance is **at least two seconds behind the vehicle in front of you**.

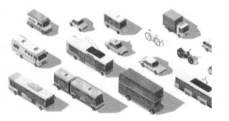

VULNERABLE ROAD USERS

Sharing the road with pedestrians

When it comes to crosswalk and sidewalks pedestrians have the rig of-way first at uncontrolled intersections and almost all the ca in the controlled intersection. Pedestrians are most at risk when they are crossing the street in trafl

crossing the street at an angle and walking along the side of the road.

The most important thing to know as a driver is that stopping on the pedestrian crosswalk is strictly illegal as it forces pedestrians to walk around your vehicle out into moving traffic. you need to stop behind the white stop marks to allow plenty of room for pedestrians to get through. As you are coming up to a crosswalk you need to be paying attention is there a pedestrian at the edge of the crosswalk getting ready to enter or from the other side of the street crossing. You still need to be slowing down and stopping if necessary even though we are at the opposite direction of traffic.

Another key to pedestrian safety is eye contact between both the pedestrian and the vehicle.

Reminder: Not all pedestrian crossings are marked, although crosswalks are present at the majority of intersections.

Driving a quiet vehicles

Operators of hybrid and electric cars should be aware that persons with low eyesight often depend on the sounds of an engine before approaching an intersection. Because a hybrid or electric car produces little or no perceptible noise while slowing or stopping, greater vigilance is required.

Sharing the road with bicyclistes

With the nice weather comes bicycles and cyclists not all of them are going to wear helmets or reflective gear so they might be hard to spot. But, be on the lookout for those vulnerable road users, as well they don't always have the same skill level. So some of them might be unpredictable and it can be frustrating, thus wait for them to clear your path and then proceed.

Bicyclists are legal drivers with laws and regulations established for their use. Sharing the road with them means mutual respect which can be promoted by public information.

Driving on roads requires care and courtesy whether you are driving a car or a bike, bicyclists have the same rights and responsibilities as motorists including the right to ride in the traffic lane when a road is too narrow for cars and bikes to ride safely side by side bicycles should take the travel lane which means riding in or near the center of the lane so here are some tips for motorists :

In the state of New jersey a 3 feet minimum of distance is required between vehicles and bicyclists.

- Stay alert and avoid all distractions while driving. And yield to bicycles when turning.

- in bad weather give bicyclists extra passing room just as you would give other motorists.

- Make a visual check for bikes by checking mirrors and blind spots, before entering or leaving a lane of traffic.

- Slow down and give at least three feet of clearing when passing reduce your speed when passing bikes especially when the road is narrow.

- And never honk your horn at bicyclists it can cause them to swerve into traffic or off of the roadway.

- Always check for bicyclists before opening your car door and don't forget that children's on bikes are often very unpredictable, therefore expect the unexpected.

Sharing the road with motorcycles and limited-speed motorcycles

Because of their dimensions, motorcycles can be hard to see, especially at night, in bad weather, or heavy traffic. They are as well more prone to injury in a collision because they are less guarded.

Motorbikes are narrow so they can hide in your blind spots or be hidden by other objects.

More than half of motorists crashes happen at intersections, scan carefully before turning left. Motorcycles are often faster than you think. You need also to allow at least three seconds of following distance when you are behind a motorcycle. Be cautious motorcycles are closer then they seem.

When motorbikes are slowing down they may use their throttle instead of their brake, so you may not see the brake lights. You need also to be courteous when you are dealing with motorcycles as road conditions affect their driving differently such as uneven pavement and slippery road.

VEHICLES THAT REPRESENT MORE DANGER BY NATURE

Sharing the road with large commercial vehicles

Driving safely in the presence of large commercial vehicles and eventually avoiding collision is the product of being familiar with their physical capabilities and maneuvers. Large commercial vehicles are designated to transport cargos and are not as maneuverable as passenger vehicles.

Large trucks have longer stopping and starting distances, they take more space for turns and they weight more. They also have serious blind spots in which your vehicle can get lost, these blind spots areas include : **directly in front, directly behind and along each side.**

You need to be careful of all large heavy vehicles that are turning, they cannot see cars directly behind or beside them. Never linger alongside a truck when passing, always try to escape by passing the truck or if it's not possible back off. pass or overtake a truck with care.

Try not to pass or overtake a truck on the left hand side, this is because a truck blind spots on the left runs down the left of the trailer and extends out three lanes. for all turning vehicles the rear wheels follow a shorter path than the front wheels, this is why truck drivers must often swing wide to complete a right or left.

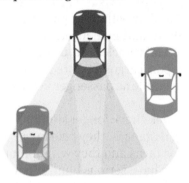

when a long vehicle is turning and displays a sign, you must not pass on the left if it is turning left or on the right if it is turning right.

Always give a room for doubt, if you think the truck is turning right wait a second and check the turning signals again the driver may actually be turning left. Also be aware of oncoming large vehicles that are turning, leave enough room for them to complete their turn by slowing down or stopping.

Large vehicle stopping

Large commercial vehicles need a significantly larger braking distance than regular vehicles. When overtaking a huge vehicle, avoid getting in front of it. This is not only impolite, but it is also hazardous since it increases the safe distance required for huge cars to brake in time.

Therefore ,when overtaking a huge car, make sure you have extra space to do so.

Overtaking slow moving vehicles

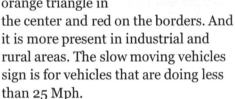

The slow moving vehicle sign is an orange triangle in the center and red on the borders. And it is more present in industrial and rural areas. The slow moving vehicles sign is for vehicles that are doing less than 25 Mph.

These slow moving vehicles which can be either farm equipment, horse drawn vehicles if you are in an industrial area these will be the industrial equipment or if you are around a marine environment other type of slow moving vehicles will be there, and you will need to know how to handle this and identify this sign.

Sometimes vehicles with that sign move over to the shoulder of the road and sometimes they don't. If they stay on the roadway, you will have to pass , and you need to be careful when you are passing because it is one of the highest risk crashes. Take into consideration road markings as well, they will give you an indication whether it is safe to pass or not. And if you are not comfortable with the gap, work with a veteran driver that can help you out with judging the gap to be able to pass safely.

STOPPING DISTANCE:

Stopping in intersections

Your stopping distance is the distance that you leave between yourself and the car in front of you when you stop in traffic or behind traffic. It is very important to keep the proper gap between your car and other cars in order to keep you and other road users safe as there will be always things on the road that you can't plan for. For some road users not obeying the safe distance rules make them think that they are keeping the road less congested because more cars can fit on a road if they keep the gap smaller, which is not the best defensive driving decision.

When stopping at intersections make sure to keep an adequate gap, this means you will be able to see the tires on the surface of the car in front of you, if you are behind a large vehicle you may need to let a larger gap to have more clear vision and time to anticipate what is coming up.

Stopping while travelling

In many cases, drivers do not realize how long it takes to stop while travelling at a certain speed. Stopping distances can come to a matter of seconds that determine if you will be able to a full stop or not in time of hazard.

Calculating stopping distance :

It is a better practice to calculate the distance and time required to stop the vehicle.

This practice can reduce the risk of an accident if made correctly, while getting more experienced as a driver this will become a second nature, that's why experienced drivers brake on time.

You can estimate the elements that enable a total stopping distance via the following formula :

	Perception distance
+	**Reaction distance**
+	**Braking distance**
=	**TOTAL STOPPING DISTANCE**

Perception time :

Perception time is the time it takes a driver to understand a situation and realize he needs to stop.

Human reflexes and judgments upon encountering a certain situation varies from one person to another. Normally, It takes drivers approximately 1.5 seconds to see a hazard and recognize it.

Nevertheless, human vision, exhaustion and impaired driving in general can significantly increase your perception and reaction time.

Reaction time :

Reaction time is based on human reflexes and their quick judgment upon encountering a certain situation. it takes generally a driver approximately one second to physically react, take their foot off the accelerator, and put it on the brakes.

However, distractions, driver's inexperience, driving under the influence of drugs or alcohol and exhaustion can significantly increase driver reaction time.

Braking time

A vehicle's braking time is determined by the time it takes the vehicle to stop once applying the brakes. The total distance travelled by the vehicle during this time period is considered as the braking distance.

In this case, the speed of travelling, the condition of your vehicle tires and tires play a major role in extending the braking time.

When stopping, begin braking early. If you brake too late, your braking distance may not be sufficient.

Release pressure on the accelerator before applying the brake to reduce your speed.

To finish braking smoothly, release pressure on the brake pedal slightly and then reapply pressure on the pedal just before you come to a stop

This means the Total Driver stopping time, on average, can be **2.5 seconds.**

ANTI-LOCK BRAKES

Anti-lock brakes (ABS) prevent wheel lock-up, especially if the steer tires in an emergency braking situation, essentially they will release the brakes.

The way that you would know that your vehicle has ABS brakes or if they are still working is by checking your dashboard, the ABS lights should come momentarily. Actually in this day and age of motor vehicles it would be somewhat surprising if your vehicle isn't equipped with ABS brakes.

The ABS brakes don't stop you in short distances, they are effective for strong brakes and in slippery roads as well so when there is snow or rain outside, ABS brakes will engage much more quickly and are prone to doing that on slippery conditions a lot more than on dry pavement.

Push hard, hold the brake pedal to the full capacity and look in the direction you want the vehicle to go to. After the execution, you can hear a noise and the shutter (grinding noise and you can feel the vehicle pulsating) and that is the ABS brake engaging.

Avoid distracted driving

Distracted traffic is one of the most common causes of crashes, stay focused. Avoid distractions that take your mind off driving or your eyes of the road.

9 Section 1 Road Signs

This 150 Road Signs Questions are Designed to be The most Closest to The Real New Jersey MVC Knowledge Test

Q1/ This Traffic Sign Indicates That:

1- No left turn is allowed
2- U-Turn is not allowed
3- A U-Turn is allowed only if there is no traffic jam

Q2/ This Traffic Sign Indicates That:

1- Children are playing in a residential area and to drive safely
2- You are entering a school zone
3- Direction sign for employees

Q3/This Traffic Sign Indicates:

1- A housing Area
2- A helicopter Airport
3- A hospital

NO STANDING ANY TIME

Q4/ This Traffic Sign Indicates That:

1- No bicycles are authorized on this road at any time
2- Do not stand or stop in this area
3- School area

Q5/ This Traffic Sign Indicates That:

1- A Zoo is ahead
2- Hunting animals is permitted in this area
3- Deer regularly cross, be alert for animals

Q6/ This Traffic Sign Indicates That:

1- A road turns right then left
2- You need to keep right of the obstacle (median, traffic island, etc.)
3- A winding road is ahead

Q7/ This Traffic Sign Indicates That:

1- You cannot enter
2- An uncontrolled intersection is ahead
3- A railroad crossing is ahead

Q8/ This Traffic Sign Indicates:

1- A regulatory sign
2- A warning sign
3- A sign for temporary conditions

Q9/ This Traffic Sign Indicates That:

1- Workers on the road ahead symbol
2- This is a construction sign, slow down and obey the flagman's direction
3- A construction sign replacing flagman on duty

KEEP RIGHT

Q10/ This Traffic Sign Indicates:

1- Drive to the right
2- Right turn yield
3- Slower traffic you should move to the right

Q11/ This Traffic Sign Indicate:

1- No parking is allowed starting at the arrows to the corner
2- A lane usage road sign authorizing right turn only
3- A lane usage road sign allowing all turns

Q12/ This Traffic Sign Indicates That:

1- A stop sign is located 150 metres ahead
2- A bump is located 120 metres ahead
3- A stoplight is ahead

Q13/ This Traffic Sign Indicates That:

1- Bicycles are authorized on this road
2- No bicycles are allowed on this road
3- Vehicle stopping is not allowed

Q14/ This Traffic Sign Indicates That:

1- A stop sign is ahead, slow down, drive through the intersection with caution if you see other vehicles
2- You need to slow down, if it's necessary, yield right of way to approaching vehicles
3- You should stop and yield the right-of-way to passing vehicles from both directions

Q15/ This Traffic Sign Indicates That:

1- Slippery conditions occur when wet
2- You must share the road with oncoming traffic
3- You need to drive with caution

Q16/ This Traffic Sign Indicates That:

1- An intersection is ahead
2- A narrow road is ahead
3- A railway crossing is ahead

Q17/ This Traffic Sign Indicates:

1- Route to airport
2- Air show ahead
3- Airplane landing

Q18/ This Traffic Sign Indicates That:

1- Speed limit on a route
2- Us numbered route sign
3- Speed limit on a highway

Q19/ This Traffic Sign Indicates That:

1- Alert slow-moving vehicle
2- A dead-end street is ahead
3- A yield is ahead

Q20/ This Traffic Sign Indicates That:

1- Pavement is grooved
2- Construction zone
3- No passing

Q21/ This Traffic Sign Indicates That:

1- An intersection is straight ahead
2- A right turn is not allowed
3- Driving straight through the intersection isn't permitted

Q22/ This Traffic Sign Indicates That:

1- *Idling is permitted*
2- *No stopping for more than 5 minutes*
3- *No idling for more than 5 minutes*

Q23/ This Traffic Sign Indicates That:

1- No passing
2- Temporarily sign
3- All of the above

Q24/ This Traffic Sign Indicates:

1- *A direction to nearby towns and cities*
2- *An upcoming roundabout and information about directions*
3- *Distances to neighbouring towns*

Q25/ This Traffic Sign Indicates That:

1- No U-turns are allowed
2- A hidden intersection is ahead
3- Lane merging from the right side, vehicles coming from both roads are equally responsible to merge correctly

Q26/ This Traffic Sign Indicates That:

1- The driver must turn right
2- Traffic may only travel in one direction
3- Keep to the right of the traffic island

Q27/ This Traffic Sign Indicates That:

1- A school zone area
2- A pedestrian crosswalk
3- Rest area ahead

Q28/ This Traffic Sign Indicates That:

1- Electric charging vehicle station
2- Electric charging phone station
3- Fuel station

Q29/ This Traffic Sign Indicates That:

1- The road ahead is separated by a median; keep to the right
2- A narrow bridge is ahead
3- A divided highway begins

Q30/ This Traffic Sign Indicate:

1- No Littering is allowed
2- A Ramp is closed
4- No Hitchhiking

Q31/ Does This Traffic Sign Indicates That :

1- The Pavement narrows ahead, drive safely

2- A right lane end is ahead; in case you drive In the right lane, you need to merge with traffic into the left

3- Divided highway ends, you should know that traffic travels in both directions

Q33/ This Traffic Sign Indicates That:

1- Roundabout ahead
2- Do not enter this road
3- Two-way road

Q35/ This Traffic Sign Indicates That:

1- The ending of a high occupency vehicle lane
2- HOV lane
3- Two way street ends

Q37/ This Traffic Sign Indicates That:

1- A road becomes slippery when wet
2- A winding road is ahead
3- A narrow road is ahead

Q39/ This Traffic Sign Indicates That:

1- Reserved lane for disabled persons
2- Disabeled person parking
3- You can park only for 30 min

Q32/ This Traffic Sign Indicates That:

1- A narrow road
2- A temporarily closed road
3- Drawbridge ahead (Bridge that lifts or swings to allow boats to pass)

Q34/ This Traffic Sign Indicates That:

1- Uneven pavement is ahead
2- Railroad crossing is ahead
3- No vehicles on train track

Q36/ This Traffic Sign Indicates That:

1- You may not park between the signs during the posted time
2- No parking at any time in this area
3- You may park in this area during the announced time

Q38/ This Traffic Sign Indicates:

1- The maximum speed at night is 35 MPH
2- The maximum speed on roadway is 35 MPH
3- A maximum speed limit is determined on the curve

Q40/ Does This Traffic Sign Indicates That :

1- Drive to the right
2- Right turn yield
3- Slower traffic you need to keep or move to the right

Q41/ This Traffic Sign Indicates That:

1- No parking is allowed 5.4m from here
2- A winding road ahead
3- Underpass ahead. Take caution if your vehicle is over 5.4m

Q42/ This Traffic Sign Indicates The:

1- End of a 50 mph zone
2- the maximum speed allowed in the curve is 50MPH
3- Speed limit will change ahead, to a maximum speed of 50MPH

Q43/ This Traffic Sign Indicates That:

1- No right turns on red
2- Right turn allowed on red
3- No right turn is permitted

Q44/ This Traffic Sign Indicates That:

1- A railroad crossing is ahead
2- A four-way road is ahead
3- An intersection is ahead

Q45/ Does This Traffic Sign Indicates That :

1- Do not enter the port area
2- Fire hall
3- There may be water flowing over the road

Q46/ This Traffic Sign Indicates That:

1- Parking is not authorized
2- A hazard sign, the downward line reveals the side on which you can safely pass
3- Roundabout ahead drive responsibly

Q47/ This Traffic Sign Indicates That:

1- Industrial area
2- Gas station
3- Phone booth

Q48/ This Traffic Sign Indicates That:

1- You should not enter between the times and dates mentioned
2- No buses are authorized
3- This lane is exclusively reserved for a certain type of vehicle and during certain days and time

Q49/ This Traffic Sign Indicates That:

1- The two left lanes ahead are closed
2- There is a highway with 2 left lanes ahead
3- Two or more passengers in the vehicle are required to take the left lane

Q50/ This Traffic Sign Indicates That:

1- A stop sign ahead
2- A railroad crossing ahead
3- Construction ahead

Q51/ This Traffic Sign Indicates That:

1- Watch for children crosswalk
2- During school hours and when the yellow lights are flashing obey the maximum speed limits as mentioned on the sign
4- Watch for pedestrians to drive safely at a maximum speed of 20 MPH

Q52/ This Traffic Sign Indicates That:

1- You should not stop in the space between the signs
2- You should not park in the space between the signs
3- Dangerous goods aren't allowed on this route

Q53/ This Traffic Sign Indicates That:

1- The road will end ahead, you must turn to the left road
2- There is a sharp bend or turn ahead
3- You must keep to the left, traffic must exist

Q54/ This Traffic Sign Indicates That:

1- You should not take the right-hand lane under any circumstances
2- An end of the highway is ahead you need to move to the right lane
3- Two way left turn lane

Q55/ This Traffic Sign Indicates That:

1- A right lane will end ahead
2- Passing is strictly not allowed
3- You can't pass if you are driving at a speed of 50 MPH

Q56/ This Traffic Sign Indicates That:

1- Bumpy road
2- Large trucks should drive at 8% of the normal speed limit
3- Steep hill is ahead

Q57/ Does This Traffic Sign Indicates That :

1- A divided highway begins
2- A divided highways ends
3- A bumpy road is ahead

Q58/ This Traffic Sign Indicates That:

1- A pedestrian crosswalk
2- A survey crew working
3- A person who controls the traffic is ahead

Q59/ This Traffic Sign Indicates That:

1- Deer regularly cross
2- Deer viewing area or site
3- A zoo is ahead

Q60/This Traffic Sign Indicates:

1- A permissive sign
2- A truck route
3- Dangerous goods road

Q61/ This Traffic Sign Indicates:

1- A rural region
2- A railway crossing
3- A pharmacy sign

Q62/ This Traffic Sign Indicates:

1- The speed limit on a residential or school areas
2- The speed limit on rural highways
3- The speed limit on rural Interstate highways

Q63/ This Traffic Sign Indicates That:

1- You are not allowed to go straight, only left or right turns
2- You can only go straight in the intersection ahead
3- Route ends ahead

Q64/ This Traffic Sign Indicates That:

1- Keep to the right
2- This is a guide for drivers in order to warn you of a change in direction
3- You are asked to stay to the right of the centre island

Q65/ Does This Traffic Sign Indicates That :

1- Police, mobile radar detector ahead
2- A Survey crew working on the road ahead
3- An officer who manages traffic is ahead, follow his instructions. Slowly and watch for the instructions

Q66/ This Traffic Sign Indicates That:

1- You are asked to keep to the right lane except when passing on two-lane sections where climbing or passing lanes are provided
2- A highway exit is ahead
3- A Two-way left-turn lane is ahead

Q67/ This Traffic Sign Indicates That:

1- Increased fines for novice drivers
2- It is not safe to enter
3- Be aware of pedestrians and your maximum speed allowed in this area

Q68/ This Traffic Sign Indicates That:

1- Allow space between your vehicle and cyclists
2- No motorists are allowed
3- No buses or trucks are allowed

Q69/ This Traffic Sign Indicates That:

1- Road forks to the right
2- A highway exit
3- You must turn right, the road ends ahead

Q70/ This Traffic Sign Indicates That:

1- Bumpy road ahead
2- Risk of falling rocks
3- Mountains ahead

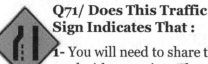

Q71/ Does This Traffic Sign Indicates That :

1- You will need to share the road with motorists, Thus providing some space
2- This is a guide for drivers to pass the sharp curves safely
3- The lane ahead is closed due to roadwork. respect the speed limitation and merge safely with traffic

Q73/ This Traffic Sign Indicates :

1- An interstate highway number
2- The maximum speed limit in the interstate highway is 60MPH
3- The number of miles until the interstate exit.

Q75/ This Traffic Sign Indicates That:

1- Small trucks only
2- No Truck of 3.5m in height
3- No trucks are allowed in this lane

Q77/ This Traffic Sign Indicates That:

1- Construction zone ahead
2- A route to avoid a construction zone
3- A roundabout exit

Q79/ This Traffic Sign Indicates That:

1- End of the road
2- Slowdown if you are a novice driver
3- End of paved roads

Q72/ This Traffic Sign Indicates That:

1- Bicycle crossing ahead
2- Bicycles aren't allowed
3- Bicycles are temporarily not allowed

Q74/ This Traffic Sign Indicates That:

1- Heavy trucks are allowed on this road
2- Heavy trucks aren't allowed on this roadway
3- Road for trucks only

Q76/ Does This Traffic Sign Indicates That :

1- A hidden school bus stop is ahead. Slow down, drive cautiously, watch for kids and for school buses with flashing red lights
2- A school zone is ahead
3- A University campus is ahead, watch out for juveniles and upcoming traffic when the stoplight is red

Q78/ This Traffic Sign Indicates That:

1- Snow may be in this area, drive responsibly
2- Road becomes slippery when wet
3- Mountains ahead

Q80/ This Traffic Sign Indicates That:

1- No Pedestrians are permitted
2- Pedestrians are permitted
3- A crosswalk is ahead

Q81/ Does This Traffic Sign Indicates That :

1- Slower traffic may be on a multilane road you must keep to the right
2- You need to follow the detour marker and keep to the right
3- Exit the highway to the right

Q82/ This Traffic Sign Indicates That:

1- Left turn is not allowed, you must turn right
2- Left turn is not allowed at the intersection ahead
3- No left turn on all the upcoming intersections

Q83/ This Traffic Sign Indicates:

1- Facilities that are accessible for disabled persons
2- Yield right of way to those with special needs
4- An exclusive lane for disabled persons

Q84/ Does This Traffic Sign Indicates That :

1- Don't pass the pilot vehicle and don't pace the vehicle bearing this traffic sign
2- Cars are not allowed in this lane
3- When flashing, you are advised to keep to the right and drive responsibly

Q85/ This Traffic Sign Indicates That:

1- Multiple roundabouts are ahead
2- A roundabout is ahead
3- A road is separated by a median

Q86/ This Traffic Sign Indicates That:

1- Be prepared to stop for pedestrians
2- No passing
3- All of the answers above

Q87/ This Traffic Sign Indicates That:

1- No littering
2- No texting
3- No hitchhiking

Q88/ This Sign is :

1- A yield sign
2- A stop sign
3- A warning sign

Q89/ This Traffic Sign Indicates That:

1- Advisory Speed Limit in the curve
2- Advisory Speed Limit temporarily on a construction area
3- Advisory Speed Limit in a school zone

Q90/ This Traffic Sign Indicates That:

1- A temporary winding road
2- A detour from the traffic route is ahead
3- Sharp curve is ahead

Q91/ This Traffic Sign Indicates That:

1- Flashing lights on the arrows show the direction of an exit
2- Flashing lights on the arrows show the direction to follow
3- Traffic keep left

Q92/ This Traffic Sign Indicates That:

1- No parking between signs includes all types of vehicles
2- You cannot stop your vehicle in this area unless you need to load or unload a passenger or merchandise
3- All answers above are correct

Q93/ This Traffic Sign Indicates That:

1- Road ends ahead
2- A roundabout is ahead
3- A stop sign is ahead

Q94/ This Traffic Sign Indicates That:

1- Multiple roundabouts ahead
2- Narrow road ahead
3- Road is separated by a median

Q95/ This Traffic Sign Indicates That:

1- lanes reserved for specific vehicles
2- Bicycles are not permitted
3- Special vehicles may take this lane either at all times or during certain hours

Q96/ This Traffic Sign Indicates That:

1- You are allowed to only park in this space during the times mentioned
2- You are not allowed to turn left during the times shown bellow
3- You are not allowed to make a U-turn during the times shown bellow

Q97/ This Traffic Sign Indicates That:

1- You are allowed to park in this space
2- You are allowed to park only for 30 min
3- Weekend parking is for fully licensed drivers

Q98/ Does This Traffic Sign Indicates That :

1- Highway ahead
2- divided highway begins
3- Road curves right

Q99/ This Traffic Sign Indicates That:

1- Offset side roads are ahead
2- Warning of one way roads
3- Hazardous roadway warning

Q100/ This Traffic Sign Indicates That:

1- Vaccine centre
2- Emergency medical services
3- Hospital

Q101/ Does This Traffic Sign Indicates That :

1- You are allowed to only park in this space during the times mentioned
2- You are allowed to park only for 1 hour
3- Weekend parking is for fully licensed drivers

Q102/ This Traffic Sign Indicates That:

1- Paved surface ends ahead
2- Pavement can become slippery when the roads are wet, you should slow down and drive responsibly
3- Pavement has been milled, thus adhere to speed limits and be extra cautious

Q103/ This Traffic Sign Indicates:

1- Mall
2- Museem
3- Restrooms

Q104/ This Traffic Sign Indicates That:

1- Hazardous material are not permitted on this road
2- A warning of hazardous montains
3- No vehicles on train track

Q105/ This Traffic Sign Indicates That:

1- This is a tow away zone
2- A construction zone
3- Machiney on road be cautious

Q106/ This Traffic Sign Indicates That:

1- Watch for people crossing your path
2- No passing zone
3- Work zone ahead

Q107/ This Traffic Sign Indicates That:

1- A construction zone is ahead
2- A bridge or viaduct is ahead
3- Bumpy or uneven road is ahead

Q108/ This Traffic Sign Indicates:

1- A Railway crossing ahead
2- Hazardous road ahead
3- You can't switch lanes into or out of a high occupancy vehicle lane in this area

Q109/ This Traffic Sign Indicates That:

1- 4-way lanes in the highway ahead
2- 4-way stop sign in the intersection ahead
3- This sign is for 4 way lanes roadways, generally found in big cities.

Q110/ This Traffic Sign Indicates That:

1- Snowmobiles parking
2- Snowmobiles may use this road
3- Snowmobiles cannot use this road

Q111/ This Traffic Sign Indicates That:

1- No left turns are allowed
2- A right turn is ahead
3- A hidden intersection ahead that may cause an obstructed view

Q112/ This Traffic Sign Indicates That:

1- Parking is by permit only
2- Person with special needs transport
3- This parking space is reserved exclusively for vehicles that display a valid Accessible Parking Permit

Q113/ This Traffic Sign Indicates That:

1- No turns on red stoplight
2- turn only if the intersection is clear
3- No left turn only in the intersection ahead

Q114/ This Traffic Sign Indicates That:

1- Y- intersection
2- V- intersection
3- T- intersection

Q115/ This Traffic Sign Indicates That:

1- Highway exit
2- Intersection exit
3- Detour marking change in direction

Q116/ This Traffic Sign Indicates That:

1- Rest area in one mile
2- Rest area in one kilometer
3- None of the above

Q117/ This Traffic Sign Indicates That:

1- Stop, then enter the traffic quickly
2- Stop, and enter traffic slowly
3- Slow down, stop if necessary, and yield the right of way

Q118/ This Traffic Sign Indicates That:

1- There is roadwork ahead
2- You must change lanes ahead
3- There is a detour ahead

Q120/ This Traffic Sign Indicates That:

1- May turn left only on a green arrow
2- May turn left on a green light when it is safe
3- Must wait for the solid green light before you turn left

Q119/ This Traffic Sign Indicates That:

1- Slight bend ahead
2- Sharp bend ahead
3- Special lane entry

Q131/ This Traffic Sign Indicates That:

1- County highway marker
2- Los angeles rest area sign
3- Services and shops ahead

Q132/ This Traffic Sign Indicates That:

1- No right turn o
2- No right turn on red
3- Only go straight

Q133/ This Traffic Sign Indicates That:

1- *A paved surface ends ahead*
2- *Do not block the intersection*
3- *Watch for falling rocks*

Q134/ Does This Traffic Sign Indicates That :

1- *Sharp right turn ahead*
2- *A road joins from the right*
3- *The road ahead turns sharply right then sharply left*

Q135/ Does This Traffic Sign Indicates That :

1- Railroad crossing, be cautious
2- Road narrow from both sides ahead
3- Road is separated by a median

Q136/ This Traffic Sign Indicates That:

1- Karaoke
2- Call center
3- Phone station

Q137/ This Traffic Sign Indicates That:

1- An intersection ahead
2- Added lane on the right right
3- an upcoming curve on the right

Q138/ This Traffic Sign Indicates That:

1- A sharp bend left turn a cross road
2- A curve left with a Cross Road
3- No left turn in the intersection ahead

Q139/ This Traffic Sign Indicates That:

1- Divided highway with light rail transit crossing
2- Don't cross the train track
3- None of the above

Q140/ This Traffic Sign Indicates That:

1- Destination sign indicating the direction to two cities
2- A reminder of the distance left to both cities
3- An interstate route

Q141/ Does This Traffic Sign Indicate:

1- This is a temporarily closed lane. You should reduce your speed to merge with the traffic in the lane that is indicated by the arrow

2- An arrow that shows highway entry

3- Temporary work on this route, please exit

Q143/ This Traffic Sign Indicates That:

1- 500 feet to until the upcoming destination

2- A distance warning

3- A tall vehicle warning

Q145/ This Traffic Sign Indicates That:

1- Side Road on the right

2- A curve on the right

3- A sharp bend on the right

Q147/ This Traffic Sign Indicates That:

1- Do not pass until after you pass the sign

2- Do not pass unless it seems safe to do so

3- Do not pass for any reason

Q149/ This Traffic Sign Indicates That:

1- Rail Transit Station

2- Railway crossing

3- Divided highway with light rail transit crossing

Q142/ This Traffic Sign Indicates That:

1- All Trucks enter ahead on the right

2- Bus entrance ahead on the right

3- Bus company on the right

Q144/ This Traffic Sign Indicates That:

1- Tourist information

2- Montain area

3- Camping area

Q146/ This Traffic Sign Indicates That:

1- A dangerous sharp turn is ahead

2- A dangerous road ends soon

3- A winding road ahead

Q148/ This Traffic Sign Indicates That:

1- center lane turn to the right only

2- Two way left turn only

3- Center lane must travel straight ahead

Q150/ This Traffic Sign Indicates That:

1- Curve and the advisory speed

2- Curve in 35 feet

3- an angle of 35 degree on this curve

PART 1
ANSWERS :

Q1/ *2- U-Turn is not Allowed*

Q2/ *2- You are entering a school zone*

Q3/ *3- A hospital*

Q4/ *2- Do not stand or stop in this area*

Q5/ *3- Deer regularly cross, be alert for animals*

Q6/ *2- You need to keep right of the obstacle (median, traffic island, etc.)*

Q7/ *3-Railroad crossing*

Q8/ 1- a regulatory sign

Q9/ *2- This is a construction sign, slow down and obey the flagman's direction*

Q10/ *1- Drive to the right*

Q11/ *2- A lane usage road sign authorizing right turn only*

Q12/ *3- A stoplight is ahead*

Q13/ 2- No bicycles are allowed on this road

Q14/ *3- You should stop and yield the right-of-way to passing vehicles from both directions*

Q15/ *2- You must share the road with oncoming traffic*

Q16/ *1- An intersection is ahead*

Q17/ 1- Route to airport

Q18/ *2- Us numbered route sign*

Q19/ *1- Alert slow-moving vehicle*

Q20/ 1- Pavement is grooved

Q21/ *3- Driving straight through the intersection isn't permitted*

Q22/ *3- No idling for more than 5 minutes*

Q23/ *3- All of the above*

Q24/ *2- An upcoming roundabout and information about directions*

Q25/ 3- Lane merging from the right side, vehicles coming from both roads are equally responsible to merge correctly

Q26/ 2- Traffic may only travel in one direction

Q27/ 2- A pedestrian crosswalk

Q28/ 1- Electric charging vehicle station

Q29/ 1- The road ahead is separated by a median; keep to the right

Q30/ 1- No Littering is allowed

Q31/ 2- A right lane end is ahead; in case you drive In the right lane, you need to merge with traffic into the left

Q32/ 3- Drawbridge ahead (*Bridge that lifts or swings to allow boats to pass*)

Q33/ 2- Do not enter this road

Q34/ 3- No vehicles on train track

Q35/ 1- The ending of a high occupancy vehicle lane

Q36/ 1- You may not park between the signs during the posted time

Q37/ 2- A winding road is ahead

Q38/ 3- A maximum speed limit is determined on the curve

Q39/ 2- Disabeled person parking

Q40/ *3- Slower traffic you need to keep or move to the right*

Q41/3- Underpass ahead. Take caution if your vehicle is over 5.4m

Q42/ 3- Speed limit will change ahead, to a maximum speed of 50MPH

Q43/ 1- No right turns on red

Q44/1- A railroad crossing is ahead

Q45/ 3- There may be water flowing over the road

Q46/ 2- A hazard sign, the downward line reveals the side on which you can safely pass

Q47/ 2- Gas station

Q48/ 3- This lane is exclusively reserved for a certain type of vehicle and during certain days and time

Q49/ 3- Two or more passengers in the vehicle are required to take the left lane

Q50/ 2- *A railroad crossing ahead*

Q51/ 2- During school hours and when the yellow lights are flashing obey the maximum speed limits as mentioned on the sign

Q52/ 1- You should not stop in the space between the signs

Q53/2-There is a sharp bend or turn ahead

Q54/ 3- Two way left turn lane

Q55/ 2- Passing is strictly not allowed

Q56/ 3- Steep hill is ahead

Q57/ 1- A divided highway begins

Q58/ 3-A person who controls the traffic is ahead

Q59/ 2- Deer viewing area or site

Q60/ *1- A permissive sign*

Q61/ 3- A pharmacy sign

Q62/ 2- The speed limit on rural highways

Q63/ 1- You are not allowed to go straight, only left or right turns

Q64/ 2- This is a guide for drivers in order to warn you of a change in direction

Q65/ 2- A Survey crew working on the road ahead

Q66/ 1- You are asked to keep to the right lane except when passing on two-lane sections where climbing or passing lanes are provided

Q67/ 3- Be aware of pedestrians and your maximum speed allowed in this area

Q68/ 1- Allow space between your vehicle and cyclists

Q69/ 1- Road forks to the right

Q70/ 2- Risk of falling rocks

Q71/ 3- The lane ahead is closed due to roadwork. respect the speed limitation and merge safely with traffic

Q72/ 1- Bicycle crossing ahead

Q73/ 1- An interstate route sign

Q74/ 1- Heavy trucks are allowed on this road

Q75/ 3- No trucks are allowed in this lane

Q76/ 1- A hidden school bus stop is ahead. Slow down, drive cautiously, watch for kids and for school buses with flashing red lights

Q77/ 2- A route to avoid a construction zone

Q78/ 2- Road becomes slippery when wet

Q79/ 1- End of the road

Q80/ 1- No Pedestrians are permitted

Q81/ 1- Slower traffic may be on a multilane road you must keep to the right

Q82/ 2- Left turn is not allowed at the intersection ahead *pass the sharp curves safely*

Q83/ 1- Facilities that are accessible for disabled persons

Q84/ 3- When flashing, you are advised to keep to the right and drive responsibly

Q85/ 2- A roundabout is ahead

Q86/ 3- All of the answers above

Q87/ 3- No hitchhiking

Q88/ 3- A warning sign

Q89/ 2- Advisory Speed Limit temporarily on a construction area

Q90/ 1- A temporary winding road

Q91/ 2- Flashing lights on the arrows show the direction to follow

Q92/ 3- All answers above are correct

Q93/3- A stop sign is ahead

Q94/2- Narrow road ahead

Q95/ 3- Special vehicles may take this lane either at all times or during certain hours

Q96/ 2- You are not allowed to turn left during the times shown bellow

Q97/ 1- You are allowed to park in this space

Q98/ 3- Road curves right

Q99/ 1- Offset side roads are ahead

Q100/ 2- Emergency Medical Services

Q101/ 2- You are allowed to park only for 1 hour

Q102/ 2- Pavement can become slippery when the roads are wet, you should slow down and drive responsibly

Q103/ 3- Restrooms

Q104/ 1- Hazardous material are not permitted on this road

Q105/ 1- This is a tow away zone

Q106/ 3- Work zone ahead

Q107/ 3- Bumpy or uneven road is ahead

Q108/ 3- You can't switch lanes into or out of a high occupancy vehicle lane in this area

Q109/ 2- 4-way stop sign in the intersection ahead

Q110/ 2- Snowmobiles may use this road

Q111/ 3- A hidden intersection ahead that may cause an obstructed view

Q112/ 3- This parking space is reserved exclusively for vehicles that display a valid Accessible Parking Permit

Q113/ 1- No turns on red stoplight

Q114/ 1- Y- intersection

Q115/ 1- Highway exit

Q116/ 1- Rest area in one mile

Q117/ 3- Slow down, stop if necessary, and yield the right of way

Q118/ 1- There is roadwork ahead

Q119/ 1- Slight bend ahead

Q119/ 2- May turn left on a green light when it is safe

Q119/ 1- Slight bend ahead

Q120/ 2- May turn left on a green light when it is safe

Q131/ 1- County highway marker

Q132/2- No right turn on red

Q133/ 1- *A paved surface ends ahead*

Q134/ 3- *The road ahead turns sharply right then sharply left*

Q135/ 1- Railroad crossing, be cautious

Q136/ 3- Phone station

Q137/ 2- Added lane on the right right

Q138/ 2- A curve left with a Cross Road

Q139/ 1- Divided highway with light rail transit crossing

Q140/ 1- Destination sign indicating the direction to two cities

Q141/ 1- This is a temporarily closed lane. You should reduce your speed to merge with the traffic in the lane that is indicated by the arrow

Q142/ 2- Bus entrance ahead on the right

Q143/ 2- A distance warning

Q144/ 3- Camping area

Q145/ 1- Side Road on the right

Q146/ 1- A dangerous sharp turn is ahead

Q147/ 3- Do not pass for any reason

Q148/ 2- Two way left turn only

Q149/1- Rail Transit Station

Q150/ 1- Curve and the advisory speed

10 Section 2 Rules of the road

This 150 Rules of The Road Questions are Designed to be The Most Closest To The real New Jersey DDS Knowledge test .

Q1/ Driving at the maximum speed limit at night is more risky than driving during the day for the following reasons:

A. At night, your reaction time is four times slower
B. At night, your braking time is four time slower
C. At night, you cannot see very far ahead.
D. Some drivers have made it illegal to drive with just their parking lights on.

Q2/In the state of New Jersey, The statutory speed limit in an urban school area a business district, or a residential area is?

A. 25 mph
B. 35 mph
C. 45 mph
D. 20 mph

Q3/ Why is it necessary to shoulder check behind you while changing lanes?

A. It will assist you in determining who is driving behind you.
B. It is beneficial for your neck.
C. Regardless of how you adjust your mirrors, there will always be an impediment
D. To see if there is unpaved surface

Q4/ Blocking an intersection during rush hours is not allowed

A. Allowed only if you entered the intersection on a green light
B. Allowed only if you entered the intersection on a flashing green light
C. Allowed on blind intersections
D. Not allowed under no circumstances

Q5/ When making a left turn from a one-way street, where should your vehicle be stationed?

A. As far left as possible
B. As far right as possible
C. Regardless of the lane
D. To the far right

Q6/ Slowing down just to look at accidents or anything else out of the ordinary

A. Prevent rear end collisions
B. Improves traffic flow by preventing accidents
C. Demonstrates defensive driving behavior
D. Causes traffic congestion

Q7/ On streets and roads, what use do broken white lines serve?

A. To facilitate the separation of vehicles travelling in opposing directions.
B. To denote a no-parking zone.
C. To divide roadways with many lanes of traffic travelling in the same direction where changing lanes is allowed
D. Separate traffic travelling in the opposite direction. However changing lanes is not allowed

Q8/ You are driving on the freeway behind a large truck. You should drive:

A. Closer behind the truck than for a passenger vehicle
B. Farther behind the truck then for a passenger vehicle
C. To the left side of the truck and pass immediately
D. To the right side of the truck and pass immediately

Q9/ The maximum speed limit for driving in ideal conditions is

A. The speed at which you can maintain control of your vehicle
B. The speed at which most other vehicles are moving
C. The posted speed for the road or freeway you are using
D. Whatever speed allows you to maintain a 2-car length distance from the vehicle ahead of you

Q10/ A flashing yellow traffic signal at an intersection means

A. You should treat the signal like a stop sign
B. Stop and wait for the green light
C. Stop. Yield to all cross traffic before crossing in the intersection
D. Slow down and be alert at the upcoming intersection, ultimately treat it as a yield sign

Q11/ Why are drivers required to use signals while turning?

A. To communicate their intentions to the cars in traffic.
B. To alert pedestrians to their presence.
C. For a better traffic flow
D. All responses are accurate.

Q12/ Does committing a moving violation in another state affect your New Jersey driver record?

A. Out of state violations affect your driving privilege but no points will be added.
B. Yes, any violation counts.
C. Luckily, no
D. Only if it's a speeding violation.

Q13/ Hands-free devices may include

A. A cell phone fitted with an earpiece or headset capable of voice dialing, or one that is connected to the car's audio system (when equipped).
B. A GPS device that is permanently mounted to the dashboard or another conveniently accessible position in the car.
C. Bluetooth earpiece
D. All of the proceedings

Q14/ Passing a motorcycle requires the following precautions:

A. Horn before passing.
B. Leave a cautionary space because motorcycle drivers are more vurnable to hazard
C. Before you pass, turn on high-beam lights.
D. Turning the emergency flashers

Q15/ What does a white arrow paint on the lane indicate?

A. As soon as the path is clear, go to the far left or far right of the lane.
B. Direction to highways
C. It indicates the point at which you must stop.
D. You may go only in the direction indicated by the white arrow.

Q16/ What is the cause of skids on the road?

A. Slippery roads
B. Acceleration
C. Outdated tires
D. All of the above

Q19/ Under New Jersey Law, what is the required distance of signaling before making a turn to alert oncoming traffic?

A. 100 feet
B. 50 feet
C. 75 feet
D. 95 feet

Q18/If another driver indicates that he intends to overtake and pass your car, you need to

A. Give the way and maintain the same speed.
B. Accelerate so he can pass
C. Move to the left to obstruct the passing car.
D. Advise the other motorist to keep a safe distance behind you.

Q19/ Driving under the influence of any medication which impairs your driving is permitted:

A. Under no circumstances
B. If you don't feel drowsy
C. If you are used to it
D. If it is prescribed by a physician

Q20/ If you are driving in slow, heavy traffic and must cross a railroad track before reaching an upcoming intersection, you should

A. Wait until you can completely clear the railroad tracks before continuing
B. Stop between the crossing gates in case they should close
C. Stop on the tracks until there is room in the intersection beyond them
D. Seek an alternate route

Q21/ If you are involved in a collision, you are required by law to exchange with the other person(s) involved your driver's license information and

A. Proof of insurance, vehicle registration and current address
B. Proof of insurance only
C. Proof of insurance and vehicle registration only
D. Address and phone number

Q22/ Who is entitled to drive first at a roundabout?

A. A vehicle turning to the left at a roundabout.
B. A vehicle turning right at a roundabout.
C. Large commercial vehicles
D. A vehicle who is in a roundabout.

Q23/ The correct hand positioning on the steering wheel when you are driving is

A. the 8 and 3 o'clock grip on the steering wheel.
B. the 10 and 3 o'clock grip on the steering wheel.
C. the 9 and 3 o'clock grip on the steering wheel.
D. the 9 and 2 o'clock grip on the steering wheel.

Q24/ If you drive slower than the flow of traffic, you will most likely

A. Interfere with other drivers on the road
B. Reduce the risk of receiving a ticket
C. Improve traffic flow
D. Demonstrate good defensive driving

Q25/ A curb painted in blue means that:

A. The space is reserved for disabled persons parking and their vehicles need to have special plates or placards
B. You have entered a parking lot at a rest area
C. That this area is a bus stop
D. You may park here for less than one hour

Q26/ In the State of New Jersey, you can drive on the shoulder to pass another vehicle on the right

A. If you are driving on the highway
B. If the vehicle has stopped for an emergency
C. Under no circumstances
D. If the vehicle is turning either left or right

Q27/ According to New Jersey Laws, a conviction of using of a handheld device while driving for a first offence will lead to

A. A fine of between $200 and $400.
B. A jail sentence
C. Losing your driving privilege
D. None of the above

Q28/ Do not make a U-turn on a curve or near the top of a hill if you cannot be seen by

A. drivers stopped on the shoulder.
B. drivers approaching from either direction.
C. drivers ahead of you.
D. drivers on your right.

Q29/ In the state of New Jersey, If you have an accident resulting in injuries to another individual while your driver's license is suspended. you may face

A. More license suspension.
B. A hefty fine.
C. A jail sentence.
D. All of the answers above.

Q30/ In the state of New Jersey, can you make a right turn at a red light?

A. No, right turns on red are not allowed in the state of New Jersey.
B. Only if you turn for an emergency
C. Only if you stop and yield to pedestrians and approaching traffic
D. Only if you slow down and yield to pedestrians and approaching traffic.

Q31/ Solid yellow lines separate

A. Traffic lanes on one-way street
B. Traffic lanes where you can change lanes or pass other vehicles
C. Bicycle lanes from regular traffic
D. Vehicles travelling in opposite directions

Q32/ What is the place where the most collisions occur.

A. Expressways
B. Intersections
C. One-way roads
D. Roundabouts

Q33/ What is the required deadline for you to notify the New Jersey MVC in case you move or want to change your address

A. Five days
B. Three weeks
C. One week
D. Two weeks

Q34/ In the state of New Jersey, it is illegal for an individual who is at least 21 years old to operate a vehicle if his blood alcohol concentration BAC is _____ or higher.

A. 0.06%
B. 0.05%
C. 0.07%
D. 0.08%

Q35/ You need to maintain a minimum distance between your car and the car in front of you

A. one-second
B. Two-second
C. three-second
D. four-second

Q36/ On a wet road, you must quickly stop your vehicle. In case you don't have ABS, the simplest solution is to:

A. Engage the handbrake and deactivate the ignition.
B. Reapply the brake if the wheels begin to lock up.
C. Only apply the brakes once even if the wheels begin to lock up.
D. Squeeze the brakes.

Q37/ When approaching a crosswalk where a blind pedestrian is waiting to cross, you must stop

A. More than five feet from the crosswalk so the pedestrian will not be distracted by the sound of your engine
B. At the crosswalk and wait for the pedestrian to cross the street
C. The law doesn't require you to stop
D. At the crosswalk and then tell the pedestrian went to cross the street

Q38/ If you feel tired while driving

A. Take a break and relax
B. Consume coffee.
C. Open the windows to allow fresh air to enter the car.
D. Have a snack

Q39/ If you're following a motorcycle, you should maintain a following distance of at least

A. three seconds.
B. two seconds.
C. four car lengths.
D. one second.

Q40/ You should usually reduce your speed when

A. Passing a large truck on the highways
B. You see brake lights coming on several vehicles ahead of you
C. You are talking on your cell phone
D. You want to look at a controlled accident scene

Q41/ In the state of New Jersey, you must register your vehicle within _____ In case you did move from another state

A. 100 days.
B. 90 days.
C. 60 days.
D. 30 days.

Q42/ Before entering a freeway, you should check traffic by

A. Looking in all of your mirrors and turning your head to look over your shoulder
B. Looking over your shoulder
C. Adjusting your side mirrors
D. Using only your side and rear view

Q43/ In the state of New Jersey the U-turns in curves are

A. Always illegal because they are dangerous
B. Always legal
C. Legal whenever upcoming vehicles are not a hazard
D. Legal only at intersections, unless a sign prohibits them

Q44/In case you did receive a call while driving your vehicle, you need to :

A. Pull over and park to respond.
B. Answer the phone only if you are expecting an important call.
C. Text back
D. Respond when the way is clear

Q45/ If you reach an intersection with stop signs on all four corners at the same time as the driver on your left. Who has the right of way?

A. The driver on your left the right of way
B. You have the right of way
C. Whoever is courteous can give it
D. Whoever is signalling to make a turn has the right of way

Q46/ Tailgating other drivers (driving too close to their rear bumper)

A. Can frustrate other drivers and make them angry
B. Cannot result in a traffic citation
C. Can result in better traffic flow
D. Reduces collisions by preventing you from being cut off

Q47/ In situations where a law enforcement stops you and ask for your permission to do something

A. You can't say no
B. You can't say no if it's outside of New Jersey
C. You have the right to not accept, regardless of what he says
D. If you say no and they say they are going to do it anyway, then you do not have a right to interfere with their actions

Q48/ A blue traffic sign marks

A. A warning
B. A construction
C. Motorist services
D. Direction

Q49/ If your vehicle starts to lose traction because of water on the road (hydroplane), you should?

A. Drive at a constant speed to gain better traction
B. Accelerate to gain better traction
C. Apply the brakes firmly to prevent your vehicle from sliding
D. Slow down gradually and not apply the brakes

Q50/ There are two traffic lanes in your direction. You are driving in the left lane and many vehicles are passing you on the right. If the driver behind you wishes to drive faster, you should

A. Stay in your lane so you don't impede the traffic flow
B. Drive onto the left shoulder to let the other vehicle pass
C. Accelerate to match his speed
D. Move over into the right lane when it is safe

Q51/ You are travelling on a freeway posted for 65 MPH, but traffic heavy and moving just 35 MPH. the best speed for your vehicle is?

A. 35 MPH
B. 30 MPH
C. 25 MPH
D. 20 MPH

Q52/ Turn on your windshield wipers and use your headlights on rainy, snowy or foggy days

A. On the high beam setting
B. So other drivers can see you
C. Anytime you want
D. Only when driving on the freeway

Q53/ When you change lanes or merge with another lane, you

A. Have the right-of-way
B. Need at least a 4-second gap in traffic
C. Should stop and check for cross traffic
D. Should rely on your rear-view mirror to determine when is safe

Q54/ You should dim your high beam headlights for oncoming vehicle or when you are within 300 feet of a vehicle

A. You are approaching from behind
B. Only in highways
C. Only in hazardous situations
D. You have already passed

Q55/ If a police officer signals you to pull over, what are you required to do?

A. Stop your car right away in whatever lane you are driving in.
B. Come to a complete stop by slowly and safely pulling over to the right side of the road.
C. You have the right to say no to the officer
D. If you find there is a valid reason, make sure to completely stop your vehicle.

Q56/ If you have a collision, the law requires you to exchange your driver license information with

A. Witnesses
B. Other involved in the collision
C. You should not share your driver license information
D. Security guards

Q57/ Safely backing your vehicle includes all the following expect

A. Looking over your right shoulder as you back up
B. Looking over your left shoulder as you back up
C. Checking behind your vehicle before you get in
D. Tapping your horn before you back up

Q58/ If your car begins to skid on wet pavement, you should

A. Slow down by shifting to a lower gear
B. Slow down by easing your foot off the gas pedal
C. Slow down by pumping the brakes quickly and firmly
D. Steer towards the right edge of the pavement

Q59/ It is night. A vehicle coming towards you has its high beams on which make it hard to see the road ahead. You should

A. Look ahead towards the left edge of your lane
B. Look ahead towards the right edge of your lane
C. Protect your eyes with your hand
D. Look straight ahead in your lane

Q60/ Diagonal yellow stripes painted on some streets and highways indicate

A. the road is narrowing.
B. there is an obstruction on the roadway.
C. either A or B
D. neither A nor B

Q61/ Which of these is the proper way to change lanes?

A. Signal, check your mirrors, and then change lanes
B. Signal, check your mirrors, and look over your shoulder before you change lanes
C. Shoulder check, signal and turn
D. Check your mirrors, look over your shoulder, then change lanes

Q62/ Collisions tends to happen when

A. All vehicles are travelling near or at the same speed
B. One line of the traffic is travelling much slower than the others
C. Where there is a traffic jam
D. One vehicle is travelling faster or slower than the flow of traffic

Q63/ Which of the following statements is true about drugs and driving?

A. Any prescription drug is safe if it doesn't make you drowsy
B. Only illegal drugs can impair your driving
C. Even over-the-counter medications can impair your driving
D. Medications do not affect you if you took them more than two hours ago

Q64/ You should use your horn when

A. Another vehicle is in your way
B. It may help prevent a collision
C. A pedestrian is crossing slowly
D. Another driver makes a mistake

80

Q65/ Driving along the rear side of another vehicle is?

A. A good defensive technique for avoiding the other driver's blind spot
B. A good way to draft off the other vehicle
C. An effective way to maintain a space cushion on your left side
D. Dangerous because you are probably in one of the other vehicle's blind spots

Q66/ Always look carefully for motorcycle before changing lanes because

A. Their smaller size makes them harder to see
B. They usually have the right of way at intersections
C. They drive too fast
D. It is illegal for motorcycles to share traffic lanes

Q67/ Before driving into an intersection from a stop, you should

A. Look left and right only
B. Turn on your turn signal
C. Look left, right, and left again
D. Look straight ahead and the left

Q68/ When may you legally go around or under a railroad crossing gate?

A. Under no circumstances
B. When you can see clearly in both directions
C. When there is no train on the track
D. When the warning lights are not flashing

Q69/ You are at an uncontrolled intersection, turning left, and a pedestrian is crossing; who has the right-of-way?

A. Anyone who is in urgency to go first.
B. Any of the turning vehicles
C. You have the right of way
D. Crossing pedestrians and/or approaching traffic from the right side holds the right of way.

Q70/ When driving a vehicle with airbags, you are safest when seated

A. At least 10 inches away from the steering wheel
B. Within 6 ½ inches of the steering wheel
C. Within 8 inches away from the steering wheel
D. Within your head positioned directly above the steering wheel

Q71/ Cargo extending more than four feet beyond your rear bumper

A. Must be marked with red flags or lights
B. Is illegal under all circumstances
C. Is not permitted on freeways
D. Must be marked only at night

Q72/ When you drive through a work zone, you should NOT

A. prepare for the unexpected.
B. watch for speed limit signs.
C. change lanes to leave more room for workers.
D. increase your speed.

Q73/ When making a left turn at an intersection or into an alley or driveway, you must yield the right-of-way to

A. all traffic behind your vehicle.
B. all traffic to the right of your vehicle.
C. all traffic coming from the opposite direction.
D. all traffic coming from the same direction.

Q74/ Drivers with an unexpired out-of-state license who moves to the state of New Jersey need to apply for a New Jersey license within

A. 60 days
B. 30 days
C. 10 days
D. 15 days

Q75/ if a turning lane is provided for vehicles traveling in both directions, you need to use

A. a left turn signal to make a right turn.
B. hazard lights to make a right turn.
C. extreme caution to make a left turn.
D. extreme caution to make a right turn

Q76/ In a typical passenger car, partial hydroplaning can begin at speeds as low as

A. 65 mph.
B. 35 mph.
C. 55 mph.
D. 45 mph.

Q77/ Which of these statements about drugs and driving is true?

A. Any prescription drug is safe to use if you don's feel drowsy
B. Even over the counter drugs can impair your driving
C. A 0.09 BAC is allowed
D. Only illegal drugs can impair your driving

Q78/ A police officer is signalling you to continue driving through a red traffic light

A. Do as the officer tells you
B. Wait for the green light
C. Treat this situation like a yield sign
D. Stop first. Then do what the officer tells you

Q79/Who has the right of way if three vehicles arrive at an intersection with an all-way stop sign?

A. The vehicle which comes at the intersection first
B. Left side vehicles
C. Right side vehicles
D. The vehicle that turns towards the right side

Q80/ According to New Jersey law, if a police officer did notice that one of the passengers in your vehicle is not wearing a seatbelt. He can write a citation for

A. Both you and your passenger
B. Your passenger, regardless of his or her age
C. Only you
D. You if the passenger is under the age of 18

82

Q81/ While driving through an intersection a red stoplight followed by a green arrow indicates that you are asked to:

A. Pass through the intersection only in the direction indicated by the arrow without stopping.
B. You can only go straight away
C. The indication of the green arrow is only for the pedestrians
D. First, you need to stop and then proceed

Q82/ When changing lanes on a freeway, you should

A. Signal for at least 5 seconds
B. Slow down before you start to change lanes
C. Sound your horns
D. Assume there is enough space for your vehicle, if you signal first

Q83/ To stay alert and avoid highway hypnosis on long expressway trips, you should

A. exercise your eyes.
B. send text messages.
C. talk on the phone.
D. take stimulants.

Q84/The roadway beyond the intersection ahead is blocked with traffic, you need to

A. keep your vehicle closer to the vehicle ahead of you.
B. Horn so that the vehicles ahead of you can move on.
C. You have the right to proceed
D. Before getting into the intersection wait until traffic ahead gets clear.

Q85/ Where there are four or more lanes with traffic moving in opposite directions, what do two solid yellow lines mark?

A. The edge of the roadway
B. The center of the roadway
C. The individual lanes of travel
D. None of the above

Q86/ At intersections, crosswalks and railroad crossings you should always

A. Stop, listen and proceed if you cannot hear anything.
B. Look to the sides of your vehicle or shoulder check before proceeding
C. Trust your gut feeling
D. Concentrate on upcoming traffic

Q87/ When you stop for a pedestrian in a crosswalk on a multilane road, you should stop at least

A. 20 feet before the crosswalk.
B. 10 feet after the crosswalk.
C. 10 feet before the crosswalk.
D. 15 feet before the crosswalk.

Q88/To help prevent hydroplaning

A. Reduce the speed of your vehicle while it is raining.
B. Make certain that your vehicle's tires have good tread depth and are properly inflated with the required tire pressure.
C. Drive with maximum speed limit of 35 MPH
D. All of the above-mentioned options.

Q89/When may you lend your driver's license to other drivers?

A. When another individual is learning how to drive.
B. Under no circumstances.
C. To anyone
D. For the purpose of identification only and in emergency situations.

Q90/ When planning to pass another vehicle you should

A. Not count on another drivers making room for you
B. Assume they will let you pass if you use your turn signal
C. Assume that they have seen you
D. Assume they will maintain a constant speed

Q91/ During a law enforcement stop if you believe your rights were violated

A. You can engage in a physical fight with the law enforcement officer if you believe he is wrong
B. You can voice an objection and file a complaint
C. You can convince the law enforcement that you did nothing even if you did an infraction
D. You can call a friend to assist you on that situation

Q92/ In cases where a traffic signal changes whilst a pedestrian is still on the street, who's got the right-of-way?

A. You have the right-of-way
B. Vehicles making a turn.
C. No one have the right of way
D. The pedestrian have the right of way.

Q93/ When parking next to a curb, you should use your turn signals

A. Only when pulling away from the curb
B. When pulling next to, but not away from, the curb
C. Use your horn while parking to alert vehicle traveling in your direction
D. When pulling next to or away from the curb

Q94/ Should you always drive slower than other traffic

A. No, you can block traffic when you drive too slowly
B. Only in the rural areas
C. Yes, it is a good defensive driving technique
D. Yes, it is always safer than driving faster

Q95/ In rain or snow, it can be hard to see and be seen. A good way to let other drivers know you are there is to turn

A. Up the instrument panel lights
B. On your emergency flashers
C. On your parking lights
D. On your headlights

Q96/ Highways are typically most slippery

A. During a heavy rain storm in the middle of the summer
B. When it first starts to rain after a dry spell
C. Anytime its raining
D. After it has been raining for a long time

Q97/ You have consented to take a test for the alcohol content of your blood, breath or urine

A. Only if you wear sunglasses
B. Whenever you drive in the state of New Jersey
C. Law enforcement are not allowed to test you under no circumstances
D. Only if a collision has occurred

Q98/ Generally speaking, you are in a large truck's blind spot if you

A. Drive close to the large trucks left front wheel
B. Cannot see the trucks driver in the trucks side mirrors
C. When you have successfully passed the large vehicle
D. Follow no closer than 10 feet behind the large truck

Q99/ There are two lines in the centre of the road to divide traffic. One is a solid line and the other is a broken line. the line on your side of the road is solid. What does this means?

A. Pass at any given time.
B. This line divide traffic traveling in opposite directions
C. It is safe to pass and overtake.
D. It is not considered safe to pass and overtake.

Q100/ If a tire blows out, you should

A. immediately brake hard.
B. immediately move onto the shoulder of the road.
C. grasp the steering wheel firmly.
D. keep your foot on the accelerator.

Q101/ On a divided highway, you must _____ unless directed to do otherwise by a sign, traffic control device, or police officer.

A. keep left of the median
B. drive on the center of the median
C. keep right of the median
D. not keep right of the median

Q102/Where there are three or more lanes going in one direction, the left lane is used by drivers who want to

A. go slower or turn left.
B. go faster or turn right.
C. go slower or enter the road.
D. go faster or turn left.

Q103/ Which of these statements are true about changing lanes?

A. You only need to turn and look over your right shoulder for lane changes to the right or left
B. Look over your right shoulder for a right lane change and your left shoulder for left lane change
C. Rear view mirrors cover blind spots
D. Vehicles with two outside mirrors do not have blind spots

Q104/ Following closely behind another vehicle (tailgating)

A. Increases fuel efficiency
B. Is a common cause of rear-end collisions
C. Helps traffic move smoothly
D. Increase visibility in fog

85

Q105/ Which of the following increases your chances of having a collision?

A. Looking over your shoulder while making lane changes
B. Continually changing lanes to pass other vehicles
C. Driving too slowly
D. Adjusting your rear-view mirror before you start driving

Q106/ If your cell phone rings while you are driving and you do not have a hands-free device, you should:

A. Answer the call because it may be an emergency
B. Send a brief text message
C. Let the call go to voicemail
D. Check the number of the incoming call before deciding whether or not answer it

Q107/In the state of New Jersey, if a driver legally changes his or her name, he/she must report the change to the MVC within

A. One week.
B. two weeks.
C. Three weeks
D. 5 days

Q108/ What is the by default maximum speed in school zone areas when there is no speed limitation sign posted

A. 25mph
B. 30mph
C. 40mph
D. 35mph

Q109/ You are driving in the left lane and many vehicles are passing you on the right. If the driver behind you wishes to drive faster, you should

A. Stay in your lane so you don't impede the traffic flow
B. Accelerate to match his speed
C. Drive onto the left shoulder to let the other vehicle pass
D. Move over into the right lane when it is safe

Q110/ You can be cited for speeding when driving 45 mph in a 55 mph zone

A. Only if you are approaching a shar curve in the road
B. If that speed is unsafe for the current road conditions
C. Under no circumstances; it is always legal to drive at or near the speed limit
D. If you are following an emergency vehicle

Q111/ You are required by the law to signal before

A. Changing lanes or making a turn
B. Entering a highway
C. In school zone areas
D. Tailgating

Q112/ You can drive with an expired driver's license within

A. 2 days prior to the expiration date
B. 3 days prior to the expiration date
C. A week prior to the expiration
D. Under no circumstances

Q113/ When sharing the road with a light rail vehicle, you

A. May not drive in the lane next to the light rail vehicle
B. Should monitor all traffic signals closely because light rail vehicles can interrupt traffic signals
C. Should not monitor all traffic signals closely
D. May turn in front of an approaching light rail vehicle at an uncontrolled intersection

Q114/ Drivers need to obey instructions from

A. Security guards patrolling parking lots
B. Flaggers at construction sites
C. Pedestrians
D. The driver of the front vehicle

Q117/ Under New Jersey law, it is illegal for someone under 21 years old to drive with a BAC of _____ or above.

A. 0.01%
B. 0.02%
C. 0.001%
D. 0.002%

Q116/ If someone is tailgating you, what should you do?

A. You need to pull over your vehicle to allow the tailgater to pass.
B. Slow down your vehicle to a certain degree so that the space in front of your vehicle could increase.
C. If it is safe to turn, move your vehicle to another lane.
D. Accelerate to match the tailgater speed

Q117/ While driving, you should look 10 to 15 seconds ahead of you

A. And focus on the middle of the road
B. Because it is legal requirement
C. Because some signs are hard to read
D. To see potential hazards early

Q118/ You are driving on a five-lane freeway in the lane closest to the center divider. To exit the freeway on the right, you should

A. Change lanes one at a time until you reach the proper lane
B. Carefully cross all the lanes at one time
C. Reduce your speed before beginning each lane change
D. Travel for at least 500 feet in each lane before moving out of it

Q119/ Under New Jersey law, you can use a handheld cell phone while driving to

A. read a message
B. make a call
C. respond a message
D. Under not circumstances

Q120/ When passing a motorcycle, you must

A. pass in an adjacent lane.
B. use the rightmost lane to pass.
C. use the same lane as the motorcycle.
D. not pass in an adjacent lane.

Q121/ In the state of New Jersey, smoking in an automobile while a child of 16 years of age or younger is present is

A. Prohibited under all circumstances
B. Legal only if it is your own kid
C. Legal when at least a window is open
D. Not prohibited by the new jersey legislature

Q122/ At what age can a child ride in the front seat ?

A. 4 years old
B. 6 years old
C. 8 years old
D. 5 years old

Q123/ When there are two or more lanes of traffic moving in the same direction, slower vehicles should use

A. the left lane, except when passing or making a left turn.
B. the center lane.
C. the left lane.
D. the right lane, except when passing or making a left turn.

Q124/ During the first 12 months as a newly license driver, you must be accompanied by your parent or guardian if you

A. Drive between 5:00 AM and midnight
B. Transport minors between the hours of 11:00 PM and 5:00 AM
C. Transport adults between the hours of 5:00 AM and midnight
D. Are an emancipated minor

Q125/ At night, if you meet another vehicle with blinding bright lights, the safest thing to do is

A. Quickly open and shut your eyes.
B. Switch on your lights on high beams.
C. Turn on your emergency flashers
D. look a bit towards the right side.

Q126/ You may make a left turn on a red light only from

A. One-way street onto a two-way street
B. One-way street onto a one-way street
C. Two-way street onto a one-way street
D. Two-way street onto a two-way street

Q127/ In the crest of a grade where your vehicle cannot be seen by traffic from the opposite direction, you cannot

A. Use your hands free device
B. Go straight forward
C. Make a U-turn
D. Make a right turn

Q128/ The total stopping distance equals the

A. perception distance + braking distance.
B. reaction distance + braking distance.
C. perception distance + reaction distance.
D. perception distance + reaction distance + braking distance.

Q129/ If two drivers enter an uncontrolled intersection at the same time, one going straight while the other is turning left, who has the right-of-way?

A. Both of the vehicles are first required to come to a halt and then proceed.
B. It's up to the driver who act first
C. The vehicle which is turning on the left side has the right-of-way.
D. The vehicle which is going straight is considered to be having the right-of-way.

Q130/ Earlier signs of carbon monoxide poisoning include

A. Fatigue

B. Headache

C. Dizziness

D. All of the answers above

Q131/ Which of the following is true about roadways on bridges and overpasses in cold, wet weather?

A. They tend to freeze before the rest of the road does
B. They do not freeze because they are made of concrete
C. They tend to freeze at the same time as the rest of the road
D. They tend to freeze after the rest of the road does

Q132/ To see vehicles in your blind spots, you should check:

A. The inside rear-view mirror
B. The outside rear-view mirror
C. You can't see them
D. Over the shoulder

Q133/ What is the difference between traffic lights with red arrows and solid red lights?

A. Red arrows are only used to stop traffic which is turning left
B. Red arrows are only used for protected turn lanes
C. You can go in the arrow's direction
D. You cannot turn on a red arrow, even if you stop first

Q134/ The posted speed limit on a road is 55mph. when the road is wet you need to

A. Drive 5 to 10 MPH under the speed limit
B. Maintain a speed of 55 MPH
C. Drive 20 to 25 MPH under the speed limit
D. Test your brakes frequently

Q135/ When making a left turn at a controlled intersection, you must yield to

A. oncoming vehicles.
B. vehicles turning right.
C. vehicles on the right.
D. vehicles behind you.

Q136/ The correct hand signal to indicate a left turn is

A. hand and arm extended outward.
B. hand and arm extended upward.
C. hand and arm extended downward.
D. hand and arm extended backward.

Q137/ You must look for bicycle riders in the same lanes used by motor vehicles because they

A. Must ride facing oncoming traffic
B. Illegally share lanes with more vehicles
C. Are entitles to share the road with you
D. Tend to draft off faster moving vehicles

Q138/ If you are the first person to come upon the scene of a collision, what should you do?

A. Ask pedestrians or other drivers for assistance.
B. Call the police and request an ambulance if needed.
C. Stop and move your vehicle off the traveled portion of the roadway.
D. Do all of the above.

Q139/ If you fail to produce the required documents to a law enforcement officer, he may

A. Take you to jail
B. Conduct a limited search for them
C. You will loose your license
D. Be fined directly

Q140/ When sharing the road with a large commercial motor vehicle, you must watch out for

A. the weight of the vehicle.
B. the side, rear, and front No-Zones of the vehicle.
C. the large mirrors of the vehicle.
D. the length of the vehicle.

Q141/ The "two-second rule" applies to the space_____ of your vehicle

A. In back
B. Ahead
C. If you are in the blind spots
D. To the sides

Q142/ Three of the most important times to check traffic behind you are

A. Backing, changing lanes, or slowing down quickly
B. Backing, making a sharp turn, or crossing an intersection
C. Changing lanes, crossing intersections or slowing down quickly
D. Backing, crossing intersections, or slowing down quickly

Q143/ When you encounter a school bus that has stopped with its red lights flashing on either side of an undivided roadway, you must

A. stop and remain stopped until the red lights have been switched off.
B. continue at the same speed.
C. slow down and proceed with caution.
D. increase your speed and pass the bus quickly.

Q144/ When you can use your emergency flashers?

A. When you see an emergency or hazard ahead
B. In an emergency stopping
C. Funeral procession
D. A, B and C are correct, thus D is the correct answer

Q145/ When you wish to change lanes, to make sure that there are no vehicles in _____, look over your shoulder in the direction you plan to move.

A. shoulder zones

B. no-passing zones

C. blind spots

D. free zones

Q146/ You can't park on the wrong side of the street or on a freeway, except:

A. In an emergency or when a law enforcement officer

B. If you are receiving a call

C. If you are in a hurry

D. A and B are both correct, thus C is the correct answer

Q147/ Unbalanced tires or low tire pressures can cause

A. faster tire wear.

B. decreased stopping distance.

C. increased fuel economy.

D. all of the above.

Q148/ In alleys, at blind intersections and at blind railroad crossings the statutory speed limit is

A. 10 MPH

B. 15 MPH

C. 20 MPH

D. 25 MPH

Q149/ A pedestrian begins to cross the street after the don't walk signal starts flashing. The pedestrian has not finished crossing when the traffic signal changes to green. You should

A. Proceed if you have the right of way

B. Procced if the pedestrian is not in your lane

C. Wait until the pedestrian has finished crossing before proceeding

D. Move to the far right of your lane and proceed as soon as the pedestrian has moved past your vehicle

Q150/ In case another car creates hazard by suddenly cutting in front of you. Which of these actions should you take first?

A. Take your foot off the gas

B. Sound your horn and step on the brake firmly

C. Swerve into the lane next to you

D. Drive onto the shoulder

PART 2
ANSWERS :

Q1/ The Answer is C. It is riskier to drive at the maximum speed limits at night than it is during the day because you can't see far ahead.

Q2/ The correct answer is A. The statutory speed limit in those areas is 25 mph unless a sign indicates otherwise.

Q3/ The correct answer is C. It is vital to glance over your shoulder while changing lanes since your rear-view mirrors will always have a blind spot regardless of how they are adjusted.

Q4/ The correct answer is D. Blocking an intersection may attract fines of up to $200.

Q5/ The answer is A. Always begin and end a left turn in the far left lane in the direction you are travelling, unless signs or surface markings indicate otherwise. To make a turn far in advance and merge into the far left lane when the path is clear.

Q6/ The correct answer is D. Do not interfere with the smooth flow of traffic by slowing down to look at an accident on the roadways. You may also prevent an emergency vehicle from arriving in a timely manner.

Q7/ The answer is C. Broken white lines (dashes) are used to divide same-direction travelling into neither one-way streets nor highways that have more than 1 lane, where changing lanes is possible.

Q8/ The correct answer is B. Large trucks has bigger blind spots. Thus, you need to drive with extra room

Q9/ The correct answer is C. The posted speed for the road or freeway you are using

Q10/ The correct answer is D. A flashing yellow light at an intersection means the light is going to turn red very soon, one should slow his vehicle and proceed with caution only if the intersection is clear from traffic.

Q11/ The Answer is D. all the responses are correct.

Q12/ The correct answer is B. According to the New Jersey Driver's Manual, conviction of an out of state driving violation will lead to two points demerits added to your driving record.

Q13/ The correct Answer is D. Hands-free devices feature all of the aforementioned options.

Q14/ The correct answer is B. Motorcycles, bicycles, limited-speed motorcycles, and mopeds sometimes need to pull to the right or left side of their lane to avoid hazardous road conditions or to be noticed by other cars. A cautionary tale about driving in the lane in question.

Q15/ The correct answer is D. You may only travel in the direction that the white arrow shows.

Q16/ The correct answer is D. A skid happens when one or more tires lose their grip on the road's surface and slippery terrains, such as a wet, icy, or snow-covered road. A large proportion of skids are also caused by driving too quickly.

Q17/ The correct answer is C. In the state of, New Jersey the maximum speed limit on urban interstates or multilane divided highways is set at 65 mph. However on rural interstates it's 70 mph

Q18/ The correct answer is A. give way and keep a steady pace until the overtaking vehicle passes your car.

Q19/The correct answer is A. Under New Jersey law, you are required to signal at least 100 feet before making a turn.

Q20/ The correct answer is A. never start a cross railroad tracks unless there is room for your vehicle on the other side. You could be caught on the tracks when train is coming

Q21/ The correct answer is A. Proof of insurance, vehicle registration and current address

Q22/ The correct answer is D. A vehicle who is in a roundabout.

Q23/ The correct answer is C. Your side airbag deploys explosively out of the steering wheel. In case your hands are higher than the 9 and 3 o'clock position. the deploying airbag could push your hands into your face, which may cause injury.

Q24/ The correct answer is A. Anyone driving slower or faster than the posted limit of the roadways may result crashing incident with cars running at posted speed.

Q25/ The correct answer is A. This is a disabled persons parking if they have special plates or placards displayed on their vehicle

Q26/ The correct answer is C. You cannot pass another vehicle on the shoulder in the state of New Jersey under no circumstances.

Q27/ The correct answer is A. In the state of New Jersey, a conviction of using a handheld device while driving for a primary offence will lead to A fine of between $200 and $400.

Q28/ The correct answer is B. Making a U-turn on a curve or near the top of a hill present a danger of not being seen by other drivers approaching from both direction.

Q29/ The Correct answer is D. Driving with a suspended license and having an accident that did lead to another person's injury will result in a hefty fine, more suspension, and the potential for at least 45 days in jail.

Q30/ The correct answer is C. Right turn on a red are allowed in New Jersey unless a sign indicates otherwise. Nevertheless, you need to come to a complete stop and give the right of way to pedestrians and approaching traffic.

Q31/ The correct answer is D. Solid yellow lines separates vehicles travelling in opposite directions

Q32/ The correct answer is B. Intersections are the most likely places for car and motorcycle collisions to occur. Typically, the car driver fails to notice the motorcycle and turns across the motorcycle's path

Q33/ The correct answer is C. Drivers who change their addresses need to notify the MVC within one week after moving.

Q34/ The correct answer is D.
Under New Jersey law, it is illegal for someone who is at least 21 years old to drive with a BAC of 0.08% or above.

Q35/ The correct answer is B.
You should maintain a minimum of two seconds between the vehicle ahead of you.

Q36/ The correct answer is B.
you should be able to stop quickly when you re apply the brakes even in bad weather

Q37/ The correct answer is B. A blind pedestrian always has the right of way at a marked or unmarked intersection.

Q38/ The correct answer is A.
Always pull over if you're feeling drowsy or uncomfortable while driving.

Q39/ The correct answer is A.
You need to let a safe distance between you and the vehicle in front of you of 2 seconds. Nevertheless, if it is a motorcycle, increase your following distance to three or four seconds to give the motorcyclist enough time to maneuver or stop in an emergency

Q40/ The correct answer is B.
When you see several cares ahead of you apply their brakes, be prepared for some hazard in the roadway by reducing your speed

Q41/ The correct answer is C. The Law of New Jersey require drivers who move in to have their vehicle titled and registered up to 60 days.

Q42/ The correct answer is A. Use your mirrors and shoulder check to get a complete view of the traffic before entering a freeway

Q43/ The correct answer is A.
According to the New Jersey code It is prohibited to make U-turn's in curves.

Q44/ The correct answer is A. for safety reasons pull over and park to respond.

Q45/ The correct answer is B.
When such a situation arises, you have the right of way as both vehicles arrived at the same time and you are on the right side of traffic.

Q46/ The correct answer is A.
Tailgating can frustrate other drivers and make them angry

Q47/ The correct answer is D. If you say no and they say they are going to do it anyway, then you do not have a right to interfere with their actions .

Q48/ The correct answer is C.
Motorist services, such as gas or pharmacy

Q49/ The correct answer is C.
Hydroplaning occurs due to build of water between road and tyre resulting in loss of traction resulting in skidding of the vehicle. To avoid hydroplaning one should gradually slow down the vehicle and disengage the brake.

Q50/ The correct answer is D.
Move over into the right lane when it is safe

Q51/ The correct answer is A. 35 MPH, you should travel at the same speed as the flow of traffic unless it exceeds the posted speed limit

Q52/The correct answer is B.
While driving in rainy, snowy or foggy weather one has to drive slowly use windshield wipers, and put headlight in low beam setting

Q53/ The correct answer is B.
Make sure that you have enough space to move into another lane without creating risk for you or other drivers

Q54/ The correct answer is A. if you are using your high-beam headlights, dim your lights for oncoming traffic and also when approaching a vehicle from behind

Q55/ The correct answer is B. do not stop immediately your car, but slowly and safely pull over to your right when you see a police officer indicating you to pull over your vehicle.

Q56/ The correct answer is B. in an event of a collision, you are required to exchange following information with the other driver

Q57/ The correct answer is D.
While backing the vehicle, one should look around the vehicle for any potential dangers to you and others

Q58/ The correct answer is B. Do not make any sudden changes in your forward motion or you could lose control of your vehicle. Allow your vehicle to slow gradually by taking your foot off the gas pedal

Q59/ The correct answer is B. To avoid being temporarily blinded by the glares of the approaching vehicle. One can pass carefully by looking toward the right edge of the road

Q60/ The correct answer is C.
Diagonal yellow striping on streets and highways indicates a narrow road or an obstruction ahead.

Q61/ The correct answer is B.
The proper way to change lanes or pass another vehicle, is to signal so that other road users know your intentions and act accordingly.

Q62/ The correct answer is D.
Collisions shall tend to decrease if all the vehicle maintains the same posted speed limit of the road

Q63/ The correct answer is C.
Even over-the-counter medications can impair your driving. Do not drive after taking any medication until you are sure how it will affect you

Q64/ The correct answer is B.
the use of horns is permitted only in situation of possible imminent danger. Unnecessary use of horn may earn you a ticket in a No-horn zone

Q65/ The correct answer is D.
Driving along the rear side of another vehicle is dangerous because you are probably in one of the other vehicle's blind spots. All vehicles have blind spots on their left sides. Do not remain in this blind spot as the vehicle ahead of you may change lanes and crash into your vehicle

Q66/ The correct answer is A.
Their smaller size makes them harder to see

Q67/ The correct answer is C.
Look to the left first because vehicles in that direction will be closest to you. Look to the right and then the left again before proceeding

Q68/ The correct answer is A.
Under no circumstances

Q69/ The correct answer is D.
Crossing pedestrians and/or approaching traffic from the right side holds the right of way. Therefore, you need to give them the right-of-way.

Q70/The correct answer is A. Air bags are safety feature that help keep you safer than a seat belt alone. Ride at least 10 inches measured from the center of the steering wheel to your breastbone

Q71/ The correct answer is A. If the load is not marked, another driver could crash into the cargo. Mark it clearly for the safety of all drivers.

Q72/ The correct answer is D.
Whenever you drive in a work zone, proceed with caution. Slowdown and be cautious of hazard and leave enough room for machinery and equipment.

Q73/ The correct answer is D.
When making a left turn at an intersection or into an alley or driveway, yield the right-of-way to all traffic coming from the opposite direction.

Q74/ The correct answer is A.
Drivers who change their name need to notify the MVC within two weeks.

Q75/ The correct answer is C. As you enter a center left-turn lane to make a left turn, use extreme caution. There may be vehicles traveling in the opposite direction that are also entering the lane to make left turns.

Q76/ The correct answer is B.
Hydroplaning occurs when there is standing water on a roadway. Up to 35 mph, most tires will channel water away like the way a windshield wiper cleans the windshield.

Q77/ The correct answer is B.
Driving under the influence of drugs is prohibited. It is your responsibility to ensure that your medication shall not impair your driving ability

Q78/ The correct answer is A.
You are expected to follow the orders of a police officer even in the presence of traffic lights and traffic signs

Q79/ The correct answer is A.
The drivers need to yield the right-of-way to the vehicle that comes first at the stop sign.

Q80/ The Correct Answer is D.
Passengers over the age of 18 are responsible for wearing their seat belts and can be cited for not doing so.

Q81/ The correct answer is A.
Pass through the intersection only in the direction indicated by the arrow without stopping.

Q82/ The correct answer is A.
Signal for at least 5 seconds.

Q83/ The correct answer is A.
highway hypnosis is a condition of drowsiness or unawareness brought on by monotony. exercise your eyes to help keep you alert. Keep shifting your eyes from one area of the roadway to another and focus on various objects.

Q84/ The correct answer is D.
Before getting into the intersection wait until traffic ahead gets clear.

Q85/ The correct answer is B. Two solid yellow lines mark the center of the roadway. Passing is normally prohibited on both sides of these lines.

Q86/ The correct answer is B.
Look to the sides of your vehicle as vulnerable road users are present in intersections and crosswalks.

Q87/ The correct answer is C.
When you stop at a crosswalk on a multilane road, stop at least 10 feet before the crosswalk so a driver in the next lane can see the pedestrian.

Q88/ The correct answer is C. All of the aforementioned options are considered correct.

Q89/ The correct answer is B.
Under no circumstances you should allow someone to use your driver's license.

Q90/ The correct answer is A. You should not count on another drivers making room for you.

Q91/ The correct answer is B. You can voice an objection and file a complaint

Q92/ The correct answer is D. A pedestrian has a right-of-way in cases where a traffic signal changes whilst a pedestrian is still on the street.

Q93/ The correct answer is D.
Drivers should turn signal when parking next to a curb or away from a curb to indicate and inform other drivers of your intensions.

Q94/ The correct answer is A.
Driving slower or faster than the posted limit of the roadways may result crashing incident with cars running at posted speed

Q95/ The correct answer is C.
Turning your headlights ON during dust/smoke/smog or any low visibility weather conditions shall help other vehicle see your vehicle.

Q96/ The correct answer is B.
Rain after a dry spell can build a film of oily, rubberish like fine loose layer on roads to become greasy and slippery

Q97/ The correct answer is B.
Whenever you drive in New Jersey

Q98/ The correct answer is B.
Cannot see the trucks driver in the trucks side mirrors

Q99/ The correct answer is D.
The solid line in the situation which is being described indicates that it is not safe to pass and overtake.

Q100/ The correct answer is C. If you experience a sudden tire blowout grasp the steering wheel firmly and take your foot off the accelerator to allow your vehicle to roll to a stop.

Q101/ The correct answer is C.
On a divided highway, you must keep right of the median unless directed to do otherwise by a sign, traffic control device, or police officer.

Q102/ The Correct Answer is D.
Where there are three or more lanes going in one direction, the left lane is used by drivers who want to go faster, pass, or turn left.

Q103/ The correct answer is B. Look over your right shoulder for a right lane change and your left shoulder for left lane change

Q104/The correct answer is B. There is no good reason to tailgate. If you follow another vehicle too closely, you will have less time to react if the other vehicle stop or males a turn

Q105/ The correct answer is B. Continually changing lanes to pass other vehicles

Q106/ The correct answer is C. if you don't have a hands-free device you are not allowed to take calls while driving. Thus, let the call go to voicemail.

Q107/ The correct answer is B. Drivers who change their name need to notify the MVC within two weeks.

Q108/ The correct answer is A. 25 mph

Q109/The correct answer is D. Move over into the right lane when it is safe

Q110/ The correct answer is B. Your speed should always be appropriate for the road conditions

Q111/ The correct answer is A. Changing lanes or making a turn

Q112/The correct answer is D. Under no circumstances

Q113/ The correct answer is B. light-rail vehicles can interrupt traffic lights. Do not proceed until the traffic signal light indicates you may proceed

Q114/ The correct answer is B. flaggers are set up by the department of transportation at construction sites for your safety and the safety of the equipment's used and the construction workers.

Q115/ The correct answer is D. All of the above

Q116/ The correct answer is B. Even though it does not seem sensible to decelerate your vehicle, as it is bound to reduce the distance from the tailgater, in reality, it will certainly allow for more room in front of you. If suddenly the car in front pressed the brakes, you will still have plenty of time to execute it cautiously.

Q117/ The correct answer is A. Under New Jersey law, it is illegal for someone under 21 years old to drive with a BAC of 0.01% or above.

Q118/ The correct answer is A. You cannot see what vehicles are doing two lanes away from you clearly enough to cross multiple lanes in one pass. Change one lane at a time

Q119/ The correct answer is D. In the state of New Jersey, you are not allowed to utilize a handheld device while driving, except in an emergency situation.

Q120/ The correct answer is A. A motorcycle is legally entitled to the full width of a lane. Therefore, to pass a motorcycle, you must pass it in an adjacent lane. You may not share the motorcycle's lane.

Q121/ The Correct Answer is A.
According to the New jersey legislature, smoking in an automobile while a child of 16 years of age or younger is present is prohibited as second-hand smoke is dangerous, especially for young kids.

Q122/ The correct answer is C. 8 years old

Q123/ The correct answer is D.
Where there are two or more lanes of traffic moving in the same direction, slower vehicles should use the rightmost lane except when passing or making a left turn.

Q124/ The Correct Answer is B.
Transporting minors is one of many restrictions placed on new drivers.

Q125/ The correct answer is C.
While seeing a vehicle approaching at night with blinding bright lights, the best you can do in that scenario is to look a bit towards the right-hand side.

Q126/ The correct answer is B.
Because left hand turns made from two-way streets must cross other lanes of traffic, they cannot be made on a red light. The only condition under which you may make a left on red is form a one-way street onto a one-way street

Q127/ The correct answer is C. In the crest of a grade where your vehicle cannot be seen by traffic from the opposite direction, you cannot make a U-turn

Q128/ The correct answer is D.
Total stopping distance is the sum of your perception distance, reaction distance, and braking distance.

Q129/ The correct answer is D.
In case the two vehicles enter simultaneously from opposite directions, the vehicle going straight is considered to be having the right-of-way.

Q130/ The correct answer is D.
Carbon monoxide is an odorless and colorless gas produced by the engine and when your windows are closed It can collect inside your car

Q131/ The correct answer is A.
Since the bridges remain exposed to cold weather from all directions, hence the bridges tend to freeze before the road does.

Q132/The correct answer is D.
Over the shoulder checking is key when it comes to making turns and checking blind spots.

Q133/ The correct answer is C.
You cannot turn on a red arrow, even if you stop first

Q134/ The correct answer is A.
Drive 5 to 10 MPH under the speed limit

Q135/ The Correct Answer is A.
When making a left turn at a controlled intersection, you must yield to oncoming vehicles and stop for pedestrians within a crosswalk.

Q136/ The Correct Answer is A.
The correct hand signal for a left turn is hand and arm extended outward.

Q137/ The correct answer is C.
when there is no bike lane, bicyclists are entitled to use regular traffic lanes. Look carefully for them because their small size makes them difficult to see.

Q138/ The Correct Answer is D.
In a situation where you are the first individual to come upon a collision, you need to stop and pull your vehicle off the road. Do not move injured persons unless there is a danger of fire or explosion. Notify emergency officials and do not stand in traffic.

Q139/ The correct answer is B.
Conduct a limited search for them

Q140/ The correct answer is B.
Large commercial vehicles such as trucks have big blind spots called No-Zones. No-Zones exist to the front, rear, and sides of the vehicle.

Q141/ The correct answer is B.
To avoid tailgating use the 2 second rule.

Q142/ The correct answer is A.
Backing, changing lanes, or slowing down quickly

Q143/ The correct answer is A. A school bus will display flashing red lights when it stops for passengers. On an undivided roadway, vehicles traveling in either direction must stop at least 25 feet away. They must remain stopped until the flashing red lights have been turned off.

Q144/ The correct answer is D.
A, B and C are correct, thus D is the correct answer

Q145/ The correct answer is C.
When you wish to change lanes, look over your shoulder in the direction you plan to move to make sure that there are no vehicles in your blind spots. You cannot see these areas in your mirrors.

Q146/ The correct answer is A.
In an emergency or when a law enforcement officer

Q147/ The correct answer is D.
they can increase your stopping distance and make turning more difficult when the road is wet. they can also cause faster tire wear and reduced fuel economy and make the vehicle harder to steer and stop.

Q148/The correct answer is B.
15 MPH

Q149/ The correct answer is C.
Do not enter the intersection while there are pedestrians in the crosswalk even if they are not in your lane

Q150/ The Correct Answer is A.
Taking your foot off the gas will allow your car to slow gradually while you maintain a firm grip on the steering wheel.

THANK YOU FOR TRUSTING US

Thank you for being our valued customer. We are so grateful and hope we met your expectations.

Remember, approach the exam with confidence and trust yourself

For more buying options, please visit ELS Series Amazon store by scanning this QR code.

Made in the USA
Coppell, TX
29 May 2023

17411780R10059